Episkopé and Episcopacy and the Quest for Visible Unity

D1509188

Episkopé
and Episcopacy
and the Quest
for Visible Unity

Two Consultations

Edited by Peter C. Bouteneff and Alan D. Falconer

Faith and Order Paper No. 183
WCC Publications, Geneva

ISBN 2-8254-1311-9

Printed in Switzerland

TABLE OF CONTENTS

PREFACE

In the search for the visible unity of the church, one of the most difficult issues to be resolved is that of the reconciliation of ministries and the reconciliation of churches which follow different patterns in the exercise of oversight. Many church union schemes have been attenuated or have failed entirely because of inability to reach consensus on these issues.

Not surprisingly, therefore, the question of the exercise of *episkopé*[1] has appeared increasingly over the past thirty years on the agenda of both multilateral and bilateral dialogues and of individual Christian World Communions. The Faith and Order Commission itself undertook a study of the topic and published a report, *Episkopé and Episcopate in Ecumenical Perspective* (Faith and Order Paper No. 102, Geneva, 1980). This study played an important role in formulating the relevant sections in *Baptism, Eucharist and Ministry* (*BEM*) (Faith and Order Paper No. 111, Geneva, 1982). Subsequently, many of the churches' responses to *BEM* raised questions around the exercise of oversight (cf. *Baptism, Eucharist and Ministry 1982-1990*, Faith and Order Paper No. 149, Geneva, 1990).

As this discussion was taking place, and sometimes as a direct result of it, some churches were considering new forms of the exercise of *episkopé* and implementing new ways of exercising oversight. They were also entering new relationships on the basis of convergences already achieved. With the ordination of women to the episcopate, a new dimension of the issue appeared on the agenda of the ecumenical conversations. The need to develop ecumenical structures of oversight has also resulted in suggestions for new shared structures, especially where there are a considerable number of "ecumenical parishes".

In the light of attempts to reach consensus and to learn from developing patterns of the exercise of oversight, the Faith and Order world conference in Santiago de Compostela (1993) called for a new study of this subject in the hope of moving beyond existing convergences. This recommendation was reinforced by two further requests for a study on this theme – from the meeting of United and Uniting Churches in Ocho Rios, Jamaica (1996), and from the meeting in Liebfrauenberg, France (1996), of the churches involved in the Leuenberg, Meissen and Porvoo agreements.

In response, the Faith and Order Commission organized a consultation on "*Episkopé* and Episcopacy Within the Quest for Visible Unity and in the Service of the Apostolic Mission of the Church" in Strasbourg, France, from 2-9 April 1997. That meeting featured presentations on the convergence already achieved, on the new relationships developed in the light of this convergence, on remaining questions which require resolution and on new developments in the exercise of *episkopé* by churches throughout the world. On the basis of the discussions of these papers the participants worked in three sections: to review new developments; to explore groundwork for theological issues; and to discuss a framework in which churches could strengthen their fellowship while still holding different positions on the issue.

It was agreed to hold a further small meeting to continue the work; and this took place in Crêt-Bérard (near Lausanne, Switzerland) from 5-11 September 1997. At this second meeting a number of presentations on issues identified at the Strasbourg consultation were discussed: the ministry of oversight; what it means to be a representative person; apostolicity and succession; and the nature and meaning of the language of "sign" concerning the ordained episcopate.

In both consultations the discussion groups produced reports. These constitute the first portion of the present volume. Editorial work after the meetings involved slight emendations for clarity and consistency of style, as well as the addition of short introductory passages for a few subsections. But no attempt was made to produce a single, harmonized report or an "agreed text".

The report of the first group at the Strasbourg meeting sets out the experience of churches wrestling with the issues for the development of their own polity, the insights of churches engaged in seeking unity in a variety of contexts as they address issues of episcopacy and *episkopé*, the proposals of churches seeking to implement structures of oversight for particular ecumenical situations, and reflections on how women exercise oversight, particularly in churches where women exercise a personal ministry of *episkopé*.

The second group report focuses on historical and practical factors leading to current perceptions and practices of *episkopé*, opportunities for advance in agreement through renewal of church life and the concept of power and its application.

The third group report reflects on the context or "space" in which ecumenical agreement is sought and provides some suggestions for strengthening the fellowship of the churches as they seek to address continuing church-dividing issues.

The three reports from the consultation at Crêt-Bérard delve further into the theological issues involved in the theory and practice of *episkopé*. They offer suggestions for addressing the issues of communal, collegial and personal exercise of oversight; continuity and *episkopé*; and the relationship between apostolicity, continuity and "sign".

The second major portion of this book consists of seven papers presented in Strasbourg. As noted, these papers and the discussions of them contributed significantly to the process of composing the group reports. Representing regional and confessional perspectives, and describing particular situations and approaches to the exercise of *episkopé*, they shed further light on the issue in general and on the Strasbourg group reports in particular.

The reports of these two consultations and the papers presented to the consultations have emerged from a process of exchange and discussion. We hope that their publication will make a helpful contribution to the discussion of the churches as they seek to move towards the recognition and reconciliation of ministries, the implementation of structures of oversight and mutual accountability, and the goal of visible unity.

Special thanks are due to Mary Tanner, Moderator of the Faith and Order Commission from 1991 to 1998, and to Bill Rusch and Neville Callam, co-moderators of Faith and Order's study on ecclesiology, all of whom lent their particular gifts of oversight to the present work on *episkopé*. The work of Renate Sbeghen in administering the Strasbourg and Crêt-Berard consultations and coordinating their documentation was also invaluable.

Peter C. Bouteneff
Alan D. Falconer

NOTE

[1] Here and elsewhere we have taken the approach of using the term *episkopé* in a way that includes episcopacy.

INTRODUCTION
William G. Rusch

Note: What follows is based on an introductory orientation presented to the participants in the Strasbourg consultation (2-9 April 1997). Before addressing the purposes of that meeting itself, it offers a short overview of previous work by Faith and Order on *episkopé* and episcopacy, a survey of *Baptism, Eucharist and Ministry* (*BEM*) and responses to it, and a review of initial steps towards a study of ecclesiology.

Episkopé and Episcopacy

It is not possible to consider the earlier work of Faith and Order on *episkopé* and episcopacy apart from its work on ministry. Faith and Order by no means ignored the topic of ministry prior to *BEM*, although there have been periods of silence on this subject – something that is not without its own significance in determining the mind of Faith and Order on this issue.

Since the origins of the modern ecumenical movement, ministry in the church has been a focal point of discussion. The inability of some communions to recognize the ministerial orders of other communions has been a principal obstacle to efforts to achieve visible unity.

The Council of Trent in the 16th century had taught the divine origin of the episcopacy, a view that finds Orthodox affirmation. The Lambeth Quadrilateral of 1888 stated the need for the historic episcopate, locally adapted in the method of its administration to the varying needs of the nations and peoples called by God into the unity of the church. Anglican views have insisted on the historic episcopate for church unification, but without resolving the question of the doctrinal foundation of the office.

Among Lutherans, views ranging from mild support to indifference to passionate opposition have all claimed the authority of the Lutheran confessions! Some Lutherans and most Reformed have rejected episcopacy because of their commitment to one ministry of word and sacrament. Here, practical as well as theological reasons may have been operative. Free church traditions have rejected the possibility of the historic episcopate in their life.

In view of this disagreement about ministry in general and episcopacy in particular, it is not surprising that the first World Conference on Faith and Order (Lausanne 1927) took up the topic of ministry. What is striking is the report of Section V, "The Ministry of Church", which notes substantial accord on five propositions:

1. Ministry is a gift of God through Christ to the church and essential to the church.
2. Ministry is perpetually authorized and made effective through Christ and the Spirit.
3. The purpose of ministry is to impart the benefit of Christ through pastoral service, preaching the gospel and administration of the sacraments.
4. Ministry is entrusted with the government and discipline of the church in whole or in part.
5. Entrance into the work of ministry is by an act of ordination by prayer and the laying on of hands to those gifted for the work, called by the Spirit and accepted by the church.[1]

The Lausanne conference recognized that in the course of history various forms of ministry have grown up, and that discussion has thus continued on the nature of ministry and on the nature of ordination and of the grace conferred. Both the function and authority of bishops and the nature of apostolic succession have been part of this discussion.

The first step towards overcoming these difficulties is the frank recognition that they exist and that they require clear definition. The Lausanne conference did not have the time to consider all the points of difference, let alone find complete agreement. It indicated that all these matters applied equally to proposals for the constitution of a united church. Thus at Lausanne there was already a perceived link between ecclesiology and ministry.

Noting that episcopal, presbyteral and congregational systems were believed by many to be essential to the good order of the church, Lausanne stated that "these several elements must all have appropriate place in the order of life of a reunited church".[2] While acknowledging unfinished work, Lausanne declared it is still possible for churches to unite in activities of service which Christ has committed to his disciples. In the notes to this report, the view of the Orthodox churches on ministry was formulated and differences among Western churches also were acknowledged, for example, the various grades of ministry and the one office, as well as various views of apostolic succession.[3]

The discussion on ministry continued at the second World Conference on Faith and Order (Edinburgh 1937). The report features comments from a number of participants who reflected on their own traditions. The general state of affairs was perhaps best summed up by the Bishop of Gloucester, Dr Headlam, who said that "the most fundamental difficulty which the conference has to face is how to reconcile the authoritative ministry, historical episcopate and apostolic succession with orders and sacraments of those churches who do not possess these."[4]

Edinburgh's Commission III on ministry and sacraments identified a number of items as providing a broad foundation for a common understanding of the nature and function of ministry. These were accepted by the conference. They were in fact quite similar to those of Lausanne: (1) ministry is instituted by Christ; (2) ministry presupposes the "royal priesthood"; (3) ordination is by prayer and the laying on of hands; (4) a ministry universally recognized is essential to a united church.[5]

Edinburgh acknowledged that different interpretations had to be taken into consideration, particularly regarding the doctrine of apostolic succession and whether or not it was the true and only guarantee of sacramental grace and right doctrine. It quoted the statement of the Orthodox at Lausanne and described the views of Anglicans, Presbyterians and Reformed.[6] It also stated that "in every case churches treasure the apostolic succession in which they believe".[7]

The final section of the chapter on ministry and sacraments in the Edinburgh report linked the form of ministry with the form of the united church of the future, thus once again placing the ministry discussion in the context of ecclesiology.[8] Edinburgh repeated the Lausanne commitment to episcopal, presbyteral and congregational systems in a reunited church, affirming that these systems would have to recognize each other's place in the church of God. Thus "the doctrine of apostolic succession would, upon a common basis of faith, attain to the fullness which belongs to it, by referring at once to the Word, to the ministry and the sacraments, and to the life of the Christian community." While recognizing that these suggestions may be unacceptable to some churches, Edinburgh was confident that where there was the will to unite, the Holy Spirit would enable the churches in coming years to improve and develop them.

The report to the churches of the third World Conference on Faith and Order (Lund 1952) stated in its section on "unsolved problems" that most of the churches believe "our Lord has called forth in his church a stated ministry. To this ministry alone the leadership of certain acts of worship is restricted." The basis for this restriction is not universally agreed upon in the ecumenical movement. Questions about the character of ministry, priestly and prophetic, continue to be grave obstacles to unity, for behind them are fundamental questions about grace and about the person and work of Christ.[9]

Later in speaking about admission to the Lord's table, the report describes the view of some "that fellowship in the sacrament rightly exists only where there is fuller agreement in doctrine, in a mutually acceptable ministry, or organic unity of church life".[10] It goes on to ask that churches which require episcopal ordination as the test of a valid sacrament carefully re-examine their practice in the light of exceptions made in limited open communion or communion by economy.[11]

In the report of the third section, on the church, the treatment of "unity and diversity" includes several paragraphs on apostolic order. This passage states that all communions possess forms of ministry and order, and that all these find sanction in the New Testament. Those who represent the catholic tradition acknowledge only the episcopal church order going back to apostolic days as wholly meeting the requirements of a unified ministry and a united church. They would regard common acceptance of a ministry in this succession as essential for full unity, although they would disagree on the kind or degree of doctrinal interpretation required. Lausanne's demand for a ministry acknowledged by every part of the church of Christ as possessing not only an inward call of the Spirit but also the commission of Christ and the authority of the whole body, is cited. The report acknowledges both the New Testament evidence and its various interpretations.[12]

The voice of Fr Georges Florovsky was heard in the discussion of "ways of worship". He insisted that the real point is not validity of orders, but the existence of the basic priesthood of the church.[13]

In the report of Lund to the churches, the chapter on "Continuity and Unity" has a sub-section on the nature of continuity. The ideas of the third section, cited above, are repeated with an appeal for a fresh start in the theological discussions on ministry. The text suggests that ministry should be seen not as an isolated phenomenon, but in the light of a profound christological and eschatological approach to the doctrine of the church. It again affirms the linkage with ecclesiology and calls for establishment of a commission.[14]

Referring to the statement on "The Church, the Churches and the World Council of Churches" adopted by the WCC Central Committee at its meeting in Toronto in 1950, W.A. Visser 't Hooft told the Lund conference:

> What we did in Toronto (and what we had to do at that time) was to relate the fact of the World Council to the existing ecclesiologies of the various churches. We sought to answer the question: how can a church justify its membership in the World Council of Churches in terms of the traditional ecclesiological convictions of the different confessions? It was necessary to ask and to answer that question. But now we have to ask the next and even more difficult question: how can we give adequate expression to the spiritual reality which exists in the ecumenical movement? And that question cannot be answered in terms of ecclesiologies which do not take any account of the possibility of such a thing as the ecumenical movement. That question can only be answered as we do a great deal of fresh thinking.[15]

In his extended introduction to the report of the fourth World Conference on Faith and Order (Montreal 1963), David Paton acknowledged that ministry had not been prominent in Faith and Order discussions for some 25 years. Yet during this period the doctrine of the whole church as people of God had been recovered, as well as a positive, creative understanding of the laity. At the same time there was a recovery of a sense of ministry in the context of mission. Together this pointed to a need for a discussion of ministry.[16]

The report of the section on "The Redemptive Work of Christ and the Ministry of the Church" affirmed the statement of the third assembly of the World Council that the unity we seek is based on a ministry accepted and acknowledged by all. The report poses a number of questions, including "Does the traditional pattern of ministry in our churches do justice to the variety of gifts of the Spirit?", "Have the churches which follow the pattern of 'bishop, priest, deacon' in fact preserved the specific character of each of these orders of ministry as taught in their formularies?" and "Do churches which have the pattern 'pastor, elder, deacon'... preserve the ministerial character of each?"[17]

The "special" or ordained ministry is set in the framework of the general ministry of all believers and developed within a christological and pneumatological framework of the nature of the church. The service character of all ministry is stressed, as is the need for a renewal of the forms and functions of ministry. Yet progress on controversial issues like ordination and apostolic succession was very moderate, and specific treatment of *episkopé* and episcopacy is lacking, though the difficulty of this topic is acknowledged.[18]

The meeting of the Faith and Order Commission in Louvain in 1971 had before it a text entitled "The Ordained Ministry".[19] This text grew out of a working paper produced in 1968 and revised at a consultation in 1970. It dealt with the source, focus and function of ordained ministry, tradition and change, authentication, and mutual acceptance of ministry. Section VII, "The Mutual Acceptance of Ministry", refers to the historic episcopate and states that an episcopal (as over against a presbyteral) church order cannot be regarded as an adequate justification for division, adding that it does not diminish the importance of the historic episcopate to say this. While "more and more churches are expressing willingness to see episcopacy as a pre-eminent sign of apostolic succession", episcopal succession cannot be seen as identical with, and embracing, the apostolic succession of the whole church.[20]

What gave added significance to the Louvain text was that it was produced with the full participation of Roman Catholic members. A revised form of the Louvain text was before the Faith and Order Commission in Accra in 1974, and after more revision became a part of "One Baptism, One Eucharist and a Mutually Recognized Ministry", the precursor to *BEM*.

Following the publication of the Accra text, Faith and Order held a consultation on "*episkopé* and episcopate" in 1979 to provide clarifying suggestions for a revision of the Accra text. The memorandum of that consultation offers an important summary of the discussion of the main issue. It links the topic of the consultation with consideration of the nature and calling of the church.[21]

The memorandum identified seven questions of special importance:

1. What is the relation of episcopal ministry to the church founded by Christ?
2. What is the relation of apostles to bishops, and in what sense are bishops in apostolic succession?
3. How is *episkopé* to be exercised in the church?
4. What is the relation between bishops in the local church and bishops exercising *episkopé* over several churches?
5. What are the functions of the bishop in exercising *episkopé* over several churches?
6. How can the past help us shape the kind of *episkopé* we need today?
7. How can mutual recognition among the churches be achieved?

Even a quick comparison of the Accra text with *BEM* shows the influence of the 1979 consultation. Clarity and movement had entered the work of Faith and Order on ministry between 1974 and 1982. All the work, drafting and discussion on ministry between 1927 and 1980 had their influence on the text of *BEM* presented to the Commission in Lima in 1982.

Baptism, Eucharist and Ministry, the responses and initial steps towards a study of ecclesiology

A revised draft of *BEM* was presented to the Commission on Faith and Order in Lima in January 1982. After considerable discussion and further revision, the Commission unanimously agreed that the text was at a stage of maturity that would allow it to be transmitted to the churches. It was an historic moment. Few at the time realized that *BEM* would become the most widely translated, discussed and commented text in the history of the ecumenical movement.[22]

BEM on ministry may be said to represent the theoretical foundation of earlier discussions and to reflect a widely discussed position, even if not to the satisfaction of all. It gives the issue of one ministry precedence over the issue of its structure, and gives priority to the apostolic succession of churches over the position of the episcopacy of the church as its sign. *BEM* presents episcopacy as an historical phenomenon of quite early origins and of some significance to the life of the church, rather than as something which dates from the apostles or which is absolutely essential to the church. It admits the possibility of diversity in the forms which the episcopate could take – a view which did not win the approval of Orthodox or of the Roman Catholic Church.[23] The view in *BEM* is that the eventual form of episcopacy as it emerged in post-apostolic times is an authentic and canonical development of apostolic ministry.

Later in 1982, the WCC Central Committee sent *BEM* to the churches for their official response. Over the next several years the Faith and Order Commission gathered these responses, eventually publishing them in six volumes.[24] The responses were also collated and analyzed; and when the Faith and Order Plenary Commission took up *BEM* at its meeting in Budapest in 1989, it made a statement to the churches on *BEM*, asked several of its commissioners to reflect on *BEM* and took some decisive steps on the way to a study of ecclesiology.[25]

At the Budapest meeting Thomas Hopko of the Orthodox Church in America reported on the *BEM* process and the churches' responses. Acknowledging *BEM* as both a promise and a challenge, Hopko noted that the responses reveal that the confessional controversies are far from dead. Differences between East and West remain, Reformation and Counter-Reformation controversies continue. Yet the context now is new. A certain growing together has occurred. Mutual influence and understanding have taken place.

Regarding ministry, Hopko noted that virtually every response commended *BEM* for rooting ordained ministry in the ministry of Christ and in the common ministry of all the baptized. Virtually all the responses agreed that Christ's church requires a special ministry of leadership. All the responses affirmed the ministry of women in the church, whatever the given church's position on ordination and apostolic succession.[26]

The Commission issued a report of the process and responses one year after the Budapest meeting.[27] It noted that while the ministry section was the longest and most difficult, it had nevertheless elicited a surprisingly large number of positive remarks. These included such observations as the following:
– even on forms of ordained ministry there is a general affirmation;
– the New Testament does not describe a single pattern for all future ministry;
– churches with the traditional pattern of episcopal structure welcome the plea for the restoration of the threefold pattern for the sake of unity;
– some churches are open to considering the threefold pattern and propose several reforms regarding collegiality, integration, and participation of the laity, while some responses oppose the normative character of the threefold ministry;
– in a number of churches there is an openness to the threefold pattern if it is kept on the level of human design and order, and not *iure divino*.

The report noted that many of the responses took up the concept of *episkopé* in relation to the function of bishops, with some asking for clarification of the relation of *episkopé* to episcopacy. Many responses accepted the distinction but not separation between "apostolic tradition" and "succession of apostolic ministry".

The Commission acknowledged that there were not many specific reactions to the section of *BEM* on the mutual recognition of ordained ministries. Some responses, mainly from Reformation churches, criticized a perceived imbalance in the steps towards mutual recognition (para. 53). Roman Catholic and Orthodox churches are not ready to move to recognition of ministries in non-episcopal churches. In the Roman Catholic Church, "the fundamental ecclesiological problem of unity lies not in an ecumenical recognition of ministry, but in recognition of the church in which this ministry is exercised as a true church confessing the faith of the apostles". Thus for the Roman Catholic Church, "it must be clear that recognition of the ordained ministry cannot be isolated from its ecclesiological context". The recognition of the ordained ministry and the ecclesial character of a Christian community are indissolubly and mutually related.

The report concluded that the deepest differences between churches are those around the mutual recognition of ministries, and that this is related to issues of the ordination of women and episcopal succession. Thus the Ecumenical Patriarchate and several other churches asked that ecclesiology be an immediate priority of Faith and Order.

The clarification section of the report mentioned specifically the need for a description of the exact theological function and structure of *episkopé* as distinguished from episcopacy. *BEM* should perhaps have expressed more clearly that the function of *episkopé* is exercised in various forms at all levels of the life of the church. It may, according to circumstances, be exercised in a personal, collegial or communal way. This function of *episkopé* is not linked to episcopacy, although many churches doubt whether an *episkopé* without bishops would meet the full criteria of apostolic tradition.[28]

Collegiality and synodality were raised as issues; and several responses noted the silence on the topic of universal primacy. Specifically, this silence centred on episcopal succession, despite the fact that most responses welcomed a distinction between the apostolic tradition and episcopal succession as an important step forward. A number of responses from the Reformed/Free Church Union were unpersuaded by arguments in favour of episcopal succession as an important element in the apostolic tradition, let alone as a condition for recognition of ministries, as some churches would demand. Thus the issue of episcopal succession remains a difficult problem. Behind it lie significant ecclesiological questions, which can be tackled only in the framework of a broader, more intensified discussion on ecclesiology in Faith and Order.[29] This study would need to involve such issues as the church in God's saving purpose, *koinonia*, the church as *creatura verbi*, the pilgrim people of God, the church as servant and prophetic sign of God's coming kingdom. Such a study should not only build on the results of *BEM*, but should try to integrate all the work done by Faith and Order on this topic. The Commission saw *BEM*'s ecclesiology as implicit and not explicit. Thus a broadly based study on ecclesiology was seen to be required.

At the 1989 meeting, Günther Gassmann, then director of Faith and Order, put forward a proposal for a study on "The Nature and Mission of the Church: Ecumenical Perspectives on Ecclesiology". It gave several reasons why Faith and Order should focus on this topic: many of the still-controversial issues between the churches have their roots in different understandings of the church; work on *BEM* was lacking a comprehensive ecclesiological framework; bilaterals were increasingly focusing on understanding the church. Stressing basic ecumenical perspectives on ecclesiology, such a study programme could provide a comprehensive ecumenical reflection on the church with all its major implications and could serve as an impetus for renewal and enrichment of the ecclesiologies of different Christian traditions. Gassmann pointed out the rich materials available, suggesting that *koinonia* could be a key concept. The final outcome could be a longer study document or a shorter consensus text.[30]

Several Commission members made valuable responses to this proposal. Here I shall concentrate on only one of these, by Metropolitan John Zizioulas of Pergamon. He underscored the importance of working on basic perspectives rather than attempting a systematic ecclesiology. Among these were the questions of the "identity" of the church, the church in its relation to God, including the church as expression of God's purpose for creation, the church as a reflection of God's way of being, and the church in the light of the idea of communion or *koinonia*.

Metropolitan John went on to speak of the structure and ministry of the church and the need to study the ministry of *episkopé* in the context of an ecclesiology of communion. This would have direct bearing on the understanding of local church, all ministries, the authority of ministry, the laity, and the understanding of the ministry of *episkopé*. "If the unity of the church in the world is understood as 'communion of churches'," he declared, "a perspective may be offered in which to place problems such as primacy, conciliarity, etc., which are still dividing the churches."[31]

The fifth World Conference on Faith and Order (Santiago de Compostela 1993) made clear its view that further work was required on the ecclesiology underlying *BEM*.[32] It noted that when questions are raised about baptismal recognition, for example, the ecclesial implications of this cannot be avoided. Similarly, the world conference pointed to the ecclesial dimensions of a number of key issues on ministry that needed additional work, including (1) the baptismal basis of all Christian ministry; (2) the nature and function of ordained ministry; (3) the question (for some) of the ordination of women; (4) the ministry of oversight; and (5) the primatial office. The conference specifically requested work on such topics as (1) how the gifts of baptism relate to the functions of ministry; (2) participation of the churches in each other's ordinations; (3) how churches authorize ministry and presidency at the eucharist; and (4) the role and significance of the diaconate.

The Santiago report noted a growing convergence among the churches regarding the need for a ministry of oversight (*episkopé*) at all levels in the life of the church. However, a tendency to identify this with the personal ministry of bishops and in particular with the historic episcopate was seen as problematic for some churches.[33] Thus the churches would benefit from joint theological and historical research into the exercise of *episkopé*. Such a study would be enhanced if carried out within the broader study of ministry in general. Here the report identified some possible topics – among them (though only briefly and in passing) the question of a primatial office.

With regard to ecclesiology, the Santiago report is more specific. It notes that the responses to *BEM* perceived the need for further work on this topic, which underlies and surrounds the understanding and practice of baptism, eucharist and ministry. It suggests that the notion and reality of *koinonia* is a suitable category for this deeper study and gives reasons for this conclusion. The evidence and the achievement of fuller *koinonia* require taking up several other issues, among them structures of mutual accountability, common decision-making and actions, forms of "local churches truly united" and "conciliar fellowship".[34]

Among the specific recommendations of Santiago was one calling for further work by Faith and Order and in the churches on the doctrine and practice of ministry, particularly noting that the topic of *episkopé* should be studied. This present consultation in Strasbourg is at least a partial response to that recommendation from 1993. It comes at a time when Faith and Order is in the midst of a study of ecclesiology, and when a number of WCC member churches have made or are in the process of making decisions about fuller expressions of unity which clearly have ecclesiological implications.

Even a brief overview of the history from Lausanne 1927 to Santiago 1993 gives evidence of a clear recognition of the importance of the topic of ministry, though not always a willingness to take it up. Up to Accra 1974, if not Lima 1982, the case could certainly be made that Faith and Order's attention to ministry was slight. The challenges of *episkopé* and episcopacy were largely left for another time. There was a general agreement that the inability of some communions to recognize the ministerial orders of others remains one of the principal obstacles on the road to full visible unity.

By the early 1980s, the situation had changed, as a result of both *BEM* and the bilateral dialogues. Progress can certainly be seen over these decades. Roman Catholics and Orthodox tend now to view apostolic succession as more than linear transmission of power. They acknowledge a more nuanced view of the historical origins of episcopacy. Some churches of the Reformation have come to a more sympathetic view of the significance of episcopacy for the consensus of the church. There is an awareness ecumenically that New Testament patterns in themselves do not settle today's questions. Ecumenical work has shown that a renewed threefold pattern will necessarily be very different from an affirmation of the mediaeval pattern. If agreement on episcopacy is not an ecumenical reality at this time, there is nevertheless greater understanding among the churches.

The purpose and aim of the Strasbourg consultation

The immediate context for ecumenical reflection on this topic at the time of the Strasbourg consultation includes several features which were not present even a few decades earlier:
1. The existence of *BEM* and the responses to it from the churches, which represents an invaluable ecumenical resource.
2. The reflection within Faith and Order on *BEM* and the churches' responses, from both the Standing Commission and the fifth World Conference.
3. The ongoing work of both multilateral and bilateral dialogues. In many of these the influence of *BEM* is obvious. Some of this work has now led to official responses by the churches. There are hints of the beginnings of reception and recognition, with new formal relations starting to be lived out.
4. The ongoing Faith and Order study of ecclesiology. Within this study there is acknowledgment that the issues of *episkopé* and episcopacy, and indeed of ministry in general, will be resolved as ecumenical issues of a church-dividing character only in the context of an ecumenical convergence – if not consensus –

about the church. As Metropolitan John of Pergamon reminded Faith and Order in Budapest, "ministries exercising authority over others must also be conceived in the same spirit of communion. The ministry of *episkopé* will have to be studied equally from such a perspective... How can specificity of ministry be reconciled with unity? How can unity and diversity co-exist? The notion of communion properly understood may be of help in answering these questions."[35]

Thus the central question before the Strasbourg consultation is: what new gleanings from the ecumenical movement – its discoveries in theology, its experiences within that body which is the church – and from the teachings of the churches on *episkopé* and episcopacy can benefit the continuing work of Faith and Order, especially its study of ecclesiology, so that these efforts can challenge the churches to see in each other the one, holy, catholic and apostolic church?

NOTES

[1] H.N. Bate, ed., *Faith and Order: Proceedings of the World Conference, Lausanne, August 3-21, 1927*, London, SCM, 1927, pp.424-25.

[2] *Ibid.*, pp.467-71, esp. p.469.

[3] *Ibid.*, pp.470-72.

[4] Leonard Hodgson, ed., *The Second World Conference on Faith and Order*, London, SCM, 1938, p.187.

[5] *Ibid.*, p.245.

[6] *Ibid.*, pp.246-48.

[7] *Ibid.*, p.248.

[8] *Ibid.*, p.249.

[9] Oliver S. Tomkins, ed., *The Third World Conference on Faith and Order*, London, SCM, 1953, pp.41-42.

[10] *Ibid.*, p.55.

[11] *Ibid.*, pp.56-57.

[12] *Ibid.*, pp.253-57.

[13] *Ibid.*, p.274.

[14] *Ibid.*, pp.25-27.

[15] *Ibid.*, p.135.

[16] P.C. Rodger and Lukas Vischer, eds, *The Fourth World Conference on Faith and Order*, New York, Association, 1964, pp.26-28.

[17] *Ibid.*, p.66.

[18] *Ibid.*, pp.61-69.

[19] *Faith and Order, Louvain 1971: Study Reports and Documents*, Geneva, WCC, 1971, pp.78-101; reprinted in G. Gassmann, ed., *Documentary History of Faith and Order 1963-1993*, Geneva, WCC, 1993, pp.116-36.

[20] *Ibid.*, p.134.

[21] *Episkopé and Episcopate in Ecumenical Perspective*, Geneva, WCC, 1980, pp.1-13.

[22] *Baptism, Eucharist and Ministry*, Geneva, WCC, 1982, esp. pp.20-32.

[23] Cf. e.g. Max Thurian, ed., *Churches Respond to BEM*, Vol. IV, Geneva, WCC, 1987, pp.1-6; G. Limouris and M. Vaporis, eds, *Orthodox Perspectives on Baptism, Eucharist and Ministry*, Worcester, MA, 1985, pp.162-63; Max Thurian, ed., *Churches Respond to BEM*, Vol. VI, Geneva, WCC, 1988, pp.1-40, esp. pp.25-36.

[24] Max Thurian, ed., *Churches Respond to BEM: Official Responses to the "Baptism, Eucharist and Ministry" Text*, 6 vols., Geneva, WCC, 1986-1988.

[25] Cf. T.F. Best, ed., *Faith and Order 1985-1989: The Commission Meeting at Budapest 1989*, Geneva, WCC, 1990, esp. pp.73-103, 201-19.

[26] *Ibid.*, pp.77-78.

[27] *Baptism, Eucharist and Ministry 1982-1990: Report on the Process and Responses*, Geneva, WCC, 1990.

[28] *Ibid.*, pp.120-30.

[29] *Ibid.*, pp.74-88.

[30] *Ibid.*, pp.202-204.

[31] *Ibid.*, pp.209-15, esp. pp.212f.

[32] Cf. T.F. Best and G. Gassmann, eds, *On the Way to Fuller Koinonia: Official Report of the Fifth World Conference on Faith and Order*, Geneva, WCC, 1994, esp. p.245.

[33] *Ibid.*, pp.249-50.

[34] *Ibid.*, pp.249-52.

[35] *Faith and Order 1985-1989*, p.213.

REPORTS
FROM THE
STRASBOURG CONSULTATION

2-9 APRIL 1997

NEW EXPERIENCES OF
EPISKOPÉ AND EPISCOPACY

Report of Group I

Introduction

In all the churches represented at the April 1997 consultation, developments in the internal exercise of *episkopé* had taken place since the consultation on *Episkopé and Episcopate in Ecumenical Perspective* (1979). There have also been developments in the sharing of oversight, some formal, others informal. And, in one case – the Porvoo Agreement between the Anglican Churches of Britain and Ireland and certain Nordic and Baltic Lutheran Churches – there has been a coming together, a reconciliation of ministries of oversight. We were grateful for the opportunity to reflect together on the implications of these developments for the move towards the visible unity of the church. We were concerned to claim together what we can all affirm in these developments and also to try to understand more clearly the areas of difference that remain between some of our churches in the understanding and practice of a ministry of oversight.

We all welcome the desire for greater visible unity reflected in part by the moves towards shared oversight. At the same time we note the difficulty that arises when a move between two partners appears to foreclose, at least in the immediate future, developments with other partners. For example, some have argued that the Porvoo Agreement between Lutherans and Anglicans makes it more difficult to envisage the reconciliation of Anglican and Roman Catholic ministries. Others see it as compromising internal Lutheran unity. We also noted that the question of coherence and consistency may be raised by regional developments within a single world communion. For example, some have questioned the compatibility of Anglican-Lutheran relations in Europe with those in the USA. This may lead to a tension between movements to unity at a regional level and the internal unity of a world communion. This makes us realize the importance of continuing the search for sufficient and required agreement in faith in the area of *episkopé* in the multilateral dialogue at a world level, for the sake of visible *koinonia* and effective common service and witness. It also raises the question of where responsibility lies for co-ordinating the theological agreements of bilateral dialogues and for reviewing the significance of the different agreements for the whole ecumenical movement. It may be that the WCC Faith and Order Commission has a greater role to play in this area in the future.

As we reviewed various developments in the churches, we noted that particular geographical and political contexts influence – sometimes consciously, sometimes unconsciously – a church's expression of *episkopé*. In other places and times a church's pattern of oversight seems to have been developed in contradistinction to secular models in a deliberate attempt not to appropriate a particular secular or political system. For example:

- in some countries which have moved to more democratic forms of government the question of lay participation in the *episkopé* of the church has been raised;
- where women's role in society has undergone a change, the place and role of women in the ministry of oversight has become an issue;
- in some countries the influence of democratic systems, slavishly copied in a church, is increasingly questioned, particularly where the "democratic way" is equated simplistically with the discovery of consensus;
- discovering consensus, under the Spirit's guidance, is increasingly recognized as not being a matter of majority vote;
- there are some places where the polity of a church needs to "fit" with the structures of society for the sake of survival, so that the church is rooted in the context and not isolated or withdrawn from it;
- the demands of mission to the secular world in a particular place sometimes provide the impetus to churches of different traditions to share oversight ministries for the sake of a strong and credible witness to the gospel.

Three areas of development

In what follows, we reflect on three areas of recent development to see what can be learned from each:

1. Developments in *episkopé* and episcopacy within churches
2. Local experiences of shared oversight
3. Ecumenical developments and proposals

Our reflections are necessarily selective and await a more comprehensive review.

1. Developments in episkopé and episcopacy within churches

Across a variety of contexts and histories, the churches are found to be experiencing developments in the ways in which they conceive of and practice oversight. Below are set out a series of snapshots of current developments in the ministry of *episkopé* from several contexts. Examined briefly are situations in newer, post-denominational churches (in China), a Baptist context (in Great Britain), two "historical" communions (the Roman Catholic and Eastern Orthodox), as well as recent developments (transcending contextual and denominational lines) in the ways in which women are exercising oversight.

a. China

In the story of Protestant and Anglican churches in China represented in the China Christian Council, we were aware that developments in the exercise of a ministry of oversight took place in relation to a powerful single-party state system where Christians needed to support each other and speak with one voice. In the formative situation described we could recognize:

– a personal ministry of oversight as exercised in the ministry of Bishop Ting (former Anglican bishop) and the two "ecumenical bishops" who were consecrated by ministers of the China Christian Council. These "personal" ministers of oversight were recognized leaders of all the member churches of the Christian Council, leaders in faith and worship and teachers of the faith. They acted as "foci of unity" for the community. In this sense their ministry was both "functional" and "iconic";

– particularly Bishop Ting acted as the link with other Christian churches, through his participation in the WCC, the Lambeth Conference, the World Alliance of Reformed Churches and other bodies;

– after the death of the two "ecumenical bishops", personal oversight has passed to two lay members of the China Christian Council. The community has "recognized" them as persons to lead because of their individual gifts. They exercise some of the functions traditionally assigned to "bishops"; however, they do not preside at the eucharist or ordain. This raises questions of the relation of oversight to the sacramental presidency of the community and to the sign of continuity in ordinations or consecrations;

– structures have also emerged of a "communal oversight" at the congregational/ local, regional and national levels of the church. The "communal" forms bring together men and women, those with oversight, pastors and lay people.

b. Baptist Union of Great Britain: General Superintendency

Baptist congregations emerged in England early in the 17th century. They were recognized as "General" or "Particular", according to which doctrine of election they espoused. Although the picture sometimes painted is one of independently gathered communities, by the mid-17th century each had given form to a sense of interdependence as truly Christian and truly Baptist.

Associations of churches formed, which gave expression to communal *episkopé*; not only in agreeing Confessions of Faith, but also in appointing Messengers, whose tasks included missionary preaching, representing the churches and settling disputes. In some cases these were recognized as having a distinct and separate ministry which may be described as "trans-local" (giving a focus to *episkopé between* churches rather than *over* them).

However, certain factors (including tension between local and wider forms of church) led to a decline in the appointment of Messengers during the 18th and 19th centuries. Still, association life remained important, in the sense of belonging together as gathered representatives and through the accepted personal *episkopé* of gifted individuals.

The 19th century saw the joining of General and Particular Baptists and the formation of a Baptist Union. Attempts were made to equip the church for mission and ministry, which included schemes for the settlement, movement and support of ministers. The resulting system of *General Superintendents,* established in 1916 and amended at intervals, eventually led to entrusting eleven ministers with the pastoral charge of oversight among ministers and their families and the churches, providing leadership to encourage Christian witness and education, facilitating ministerial settlements and acting as representatives and advocates of the Baptist Union. These ministers were to be in relationship with the other members of the Board of Superintendents and each would have the support of one Area Pastoral Committee. Actual practice could vary, as the workload remained too heavy for any individual to do justice to the whole. Questions of power, perceived power and the nature of authority have surfaced regularly.

Such questions led most recently to a formal review of the Superintendency from 1994 to 1996. Its report was significantly entitled *Transforming Superintendency.* For largely historical reasons, Baptists are reluctant to use "episcopal" language, yet the fact remains that a ministry of oversight is exercised among Baptists which needs both articulating and reforming. Among many specific recommendations, it is important to note the requirement that the churches look closely at patterns of associating.

The primary (though not sole) area of the General Superintendents' responsibilities is the pastoral care of ministers as partners in God's mission through the churches – in connection with the Associations through the Area Pastoral Committee, the theological colleges and the Ministry Department of the Baptist Union.

All this, Baptists believe, stems from reflection in their denominational context on the theological affirmation of faith in the Triune God of constant relationship, whose mission of love is to go out to all creation. Perhaps the deepest significance of this review has been the attempt to articulate the impetus this brings towards recognizing and implementing appropriate forms of *episkopé.*

c. Roman Catholic Church

While the Roman Catholic Church has always been episcopally ordered, the manner in which individual bishops exercise this *episkopé* in their local churches may vary, even according to the provisions of Canon Law. Collegial and communal exercise of oversight can also be found to vary.

Strictly speaking, collegiality in the Roman Catholic Church is an activity involving the whole body of bishops, either spread throughout the world but teaching together or gathering together in a council. Within this collegiality of the whole body of bishops there is an exercise of personal primacy by the Bishop of Rome, who has a particular form of *episkopé* as head of the college of bishops.

Since the Second Vatican Council some new experiences of *episkopé* have emerged which are increasingly collegial and communal. In larger dioceses, for example, a bishop (or archbishop) may have a number of auxiliary bishops and hence exercise his *episkopé* in a more collegial way in the local church. Within such dioceses the bishop may be assisted by a number of episcopal vicars who share his *episkopé* in various regions or areas of responsibility.

In many dioceses, there are structures such as pastoral councils or synods in which bishops consult with clergy and lay people, enabling them to have some communal dimension to their *episkopé.* At the regional level, conferences of bishops exercise a form of collegiality, although they exist more for common counsel than for direct *episkopé* over the local churches.

The various experiences of *episkopé* thus give evidence of both new structures and new ways of using existing structures.

d. Orthodox Church

The Eastern Orthodox Church is a communion of local autocephalous churches, each headed by a primate. This person, whether patriarch, metropolitan or archbishop, is an *episkopos* in a *primus inter pares* primacy of honour among the other *episkopoi* of his church, who also oversee regional dioceses. The *primus inter pares* of all the autocephalous churches is the Patriarch of Constantinople.

This structure results in a large degree of independence on the level of regional dioceses and especially of local autocephalous churches. But independence is not self-sufficiency, and the bonds of communion which unite all the local Orthodox churches are experienced sacramentally as well as through the collegiality of episcopal oversight. The practice of collegial oversight is evident on the global level in the historical ecumenical councils and in the contemporary pan-Orthodox meetings. On the local level, each autocephalous church has its synod of bishops.

The communal nature and exercise of episcopal oversight is evident in two ways: first, the election of each *episkopos* arises from and occurs within the local eucharistic community. Moreover, some dioceses and autocephalous churches feature as a part of their governing structures assemblies which involve clergy and laity.

In certain areas, particularly among the so-called "diaspora" churches where parallel jurisdictions exist, the unity of the church on the administrative, synchronic level is not evident. But these situations, which are universally regarded as anomalous, do not impinge upon the diachronic unity of the church. Thus the *episkopos* guarantees unity notably through continuity of faith and church life, as expressed (and grounded) in the teachings of councils throughout history, in the liturgy, in the church's monastic and parish life – all areas that are in relationship with the bishop.

In many areas, personal and collegial forms of *episkopé* have developed in new ways as a response to the ecclesiological and ecclesiastical problem of parallel jurisdictions. One such provisional structure is the Assembly of Orthodox Bishops of France (*Assemblée des Evêques orthodoxes de France*), whose membership comprises the bishops from every canonical Orthodox church body in France. This and similar structures in the United States, Germany and elsewhere make it evident that even within situations where the "one bishop in each place" norm has not been consistently upheld, provision is made for collegiality and conciliarity.

Concern for continued episcopal collegiality on the global level is seen today in the greater frequency of informal meetings of the heads of the autocephalous churches. It is also manifested in the character of the pan-Orthodox process which is preparing a general synod of the Orthodox church.

e. Women in the ministry of oversight

In no church are women excluded from every form of *episkopé*, although the degree of involvement in decision-making structures varies considerably. There have always been women who by charismatic and moral authority have exercised some form of *episkopé*.

In the Orthodox and Roman Catholic churches this *episkopé* is exercised in a formal way only by leaders of Religious Congregations, in which women have jurisdiction according to the constitutions of these Congregations, usually worked out in a collegial manner. However, there are also instances of women participating formally in the process of discernment required to elect a bishop, or functioning consultatively and/or critically as the bishop engages in his work. Some Roman Catholic dioceses have appointed Women's Advisors, and in some cases women act as consultants to a Bishops' Conference. In many Orthodox churches the electoral colleges responsible for the election of bishops are composed of both clerical and lay representation, including abbesses and the women directors of monastic seminaries. The tradition of lay theologians within the Orthodox church contributes to broader oversight on the part of lay men and women as theologians and teachers.

Within other churches, both episcopal and non-episcopal, there is an increasing involvement of women in the exercise of personal *episkopé*, either through episcopal roles or the decision-making structures. This is unevenly expressed in different points of each world communion. Since the 1979 Faith and Order consultation on *episkopé*, women bishops have been consecrated in a number of communions: in the Methodist church, some Lutheran churches and some churches of the Anglican Communion. In non-episcopal churches, increasing numbers of women have been appointed to oversight roles.

This brief overview may serve as a reminder that this discussion is not about whether there is a "place" for women in the church – this is not in question. Nevertheless, real differences do remain in the interpretation of the common understanding of the church as the Body of Christ, of the representative nature of the bishop as icon of Christ (*imago Christi*) and the role of the bishop as focus of unity. The decision of some episcopal churches to ordain women has sharpened the question in ecumenical discussion – moving it from a theoretical issue to a perceived anomaly or problem and, for some, an ecumenical possibility. Frustration is sometimes expressed by non-episcopal churches (among which there is still diversity on the nature of oversight and the acceptability of its exercise by women) when the very discussion in which they participate is sensed as calling into question the validity of their church order. There is an equal frustration when episcopal churches feel judged for their stance in continuing the tradition of an all-male episcopate.

In the Protestant church in China, women have been ordained during a period of rapid growth in response to the need to preserve the continuity of faith. In the Jamaican church in times of slavery, authentic Christian witness, without a formally recognized ministry, was maintained by both women and men. Recognition of factors like these may help to keep the doors open for discussion in an area threatened by deadlock.

It is clear that the matter of women in the personal ministry of oversight remains a disputed question both within and between churches. We believe that it is important for churches to continue evaluating together the theological and ecclesiological issues as well as reviewing together the experience of women in ministries of personal oversight. As was said in *BEM* in relation to the ordination of women to the priesthood: "openness to each other holds the possibility that the Spirit may well speak to one church through the insights of another".

* * *

In reflecting on these examples of the development of the exercise of oversight in different churches, we found in *Baptism, Eucharist and Ministry* a useful "key" to recognizing some commonalities between churches of very different polities. The *BEM* text talks of the "personal, collegial and communal" dimensions of oversight exercised at the local and regional levels:

Guiding Principles for the Exercise of the Ordained Ministry in the Church

Three considerations are important in this respect. The ordained ministry should be exercised in a personal, collegial and communal way. It should be *personal* because the presence of Christ among his people can most effectively be pointed to by the person ordained to proclaim the gospel and to call the community to serve the Lord in unity of life and witness. It should also be *collegial*, for there is need for a college of ordained ministers sharing in the common task of representing the concerns of the community. Finally, the intimate relationship between the ordained ministry and the community should find expression in a *communal* dimension where the exercise of the ordained ministry is rooted in the life of the community and requires the community's effective participation in the discovery of God's will and the guidance of the Spirit.

The ordained ministry needs to be constitutionally or canonically ordered and exercised in the church in such a way that each of these three dimensions can find adequate expression. At the level of the local eucharistic community there is need for an ordained minister acting within a collegial body. Strong emphasis should be placed on the active participation of all members in the life and the decision-making of the community. At the regional level there is again need for an ordained minister exercising a service of unity. The collegial and communal dimensions will find expression in regular representative synodal gatherings (Ministry, paras 26-27).

In some churches we noted that the personal, collegial and communal forms of oversight are exercised not only at the local and regional levels, but also at the world level: the personal in the ministry of the Bishop of Rome, the Ecumenical Patriarch and the Archbishop of Canterbury; the collegial in a council such as the Second Vatican Council, the proposed Pan-Orthodox Synod and the Lambeth Conference; the communal in the Anglican Consultative Council, which brings together bishops, clergy and laity at the world level. Other world communions also have communal structures at a world level – the Baptist World Alliance, the World Alliance of Reformed Churches, the Lutheran World Federation, etc. – but these are not generally given ecclesial significance.

In light of the above, we noted several points:
– All our churches exercise a ministry of oversight.
– The expressions of the exercise of personal, collegial and communal oversight differ between the churches.
– The different exercise of personal, collegial and communal oversight reflects ways in which the churches are variously nurtured in the faith, pastored, guided and disciplined.

- These forms of oversight serve the unity of churches and are "bonds of connectedness" and instruments of communion, solidarity and mutual accountability.
- The ministry of oversight in all churches, in its various dimensions, is concerned with the nurturing and maintenance of the community's fidelity to the teaching and mission of the apostles.
- In churches where the ministry of oversight entails the historic episcopal succession, the diachronic unity of the churches is emphasized in personal succession. Care for faithful continuity through the ages is shown in non-episcopal churches in the act of ordination by those who were themselves ordained in succession – as well as in the exercise of oversight by corporate bodies such as presbyteries.
- In all the churches the ministry of oversight is connected to the faithful preaching of the gospel and the authentic celebration of the sacraments.
- The way in which the churches express the relationship between continuity in apostolic faith and mission on the one hand and ministerial continuity on the other differs. Some use the language of "guarantee", others "effective sign" to describe the relationship, and still others make no attempt to explicate the relationship.
- There is a difference between churches which place emphasis upon the "iconic" or "symbolic" nature of personal oversight and churches for which personal oversight is primarily functional. However, we noted some convergence even here. For example, the Baptist Union of Great Britain in its recent report on superintendency describes those who exercise personal oversight in more than functional terms.
- There is a recognition of the positive aspects in a personal ministry of oversight at the world level. Some also cite negative aspects, particularly in relation to the claims of universal and immediate jurisdiction in the ministry of the Bishop of Rome and of papal infallibility, at least as this is sometimes interpreted and acted upon. Nevertheless, the invitation by the Bishop of Rome in *Ut Unum Sint* to engage with him in an exploration of his ministry in the service of the unity of the church was welcomed.
- The several developments in the exercise of oversight which we have noted above testify to a common concern to make the ministry of oversight relevant to the mission of the church in the contemporary world.
- Whether intentionally or not, ecumenical statements have sometimes given the impression that convergence in the practice of *episkopé* is a one-way process: namely, that churches in which *episkopé* is exercised in a presbyteral or corporate fashion need to embrace personal episcopacy. In fact, the process requires all churches to examine their practice of *episkopé*. Non-episcopal churches need to consider the merits of a personal episcopate; churches which are episcopally ordered are challenged to seek the renewal of their practice of episcopal ministry, taking into account the positive contributions which can be made by systems of presbyteral and corporate oversight. A frank acceptance by all parties of the need for renewal and mutual enrichment will do much to remove negative perceptions and to advance *koinonia* and the process of convergence.

2. Local experiences of shared oversight

In some parts of the world, Christians in the same town or local area but from different traditions are beginning to develop new ways of becoming the "all in each place" envisaged at the WCC's third assembly (New Delhi 1961). The experimental nature of these partnerships was reflected in the title used in England in the 1970s: "Areas of Ecumenical Experiment". For some, the more recently adopted title "Local Ecumenical Partnerships" tends to obscure the fact that these new partnerships make sense only within an overall commitment of the participating churches themselves to move beyond the present situation to the visible unity of the church – from the "all in each place" to "all in every place". Local partnerships need to be understood as a vital stage on the way to the visible unity of the whole church.

In England, "Local Ecumenical Partnership" (LEP) is used for a variety of patterns of ecumenical life: a united congregation, a shared building, the grouping together of congregations of a number of traditions with a covenanted shared life of mission, shared chaplaincies. The 800 or more LEPs, which differ from one another, are constituted formally by the participating traditions. The participation of the Church of England in LEPs is governed by Ecumenical Canons which set out the degree of shared worship and shared ministry which a bishop may permit in any particular LEP. The churches involved in these partnerships include Anglican, Baptist, Methodist, United Reformed, Moravian, Roman Catholic and some House Churches. The degree of shared life differs from LEP to LEP according to the partners involved and according to what is set out in the formal sharing agreement. LEPs are motivated by the concern for the unity and mission of the church. The shared life may include the regular celebration of common worship, including the celebration of baptism, joint confirmations, eucharistic hospitality (though not when a partnership involves Roman Catholics), a degree of shared ministry, though for Anglicans and Roman Catholics there is not an interchangeable ministry.

In Wales, "Local Ecumenical Projects" are local united congregations or groups of congregations in covenant. Ireland has a number of shared buildings, while in Scotland there is a mix of united congregations and shared buildings. Aotearoa-New Zealand has "Co-operative Ventures" and "Co-operating Parishes"; in South Africa there are united congregations; the Caribbean countries and Canada speak of "shared ministries". In Australia there are a number of developing covenants.

A more recent development emerging in New Zealand, Wales and England is new forms of joint oversight. In New Zealand there are Joint Regional Councils which take responsibility for Co-operative Ventures. In England every formally constituted LEP is overseen by a Sponsoring Body made up of members of the participating churches and having an ongoing responsibility for the care of one or more LEPs. The leaders of the participating churches (Chairmen of Districts, Bishops, etc.) delegate certain of their functions of oversight to be carried out by the Sponsoring Bodies, which regularly review the life, including the liturgical life, of the LEP. The Sponsoring Body is accountable to the parent churches.

Out of the grouping together of a number of LEPs in the new town of Milton Keynes, England, the need arose for a person to oversee these ecumenical partnerships, and an Ecumenical Moderator was appointed. In Wales there is currently a proposal before the Welsh churches to establish an Ecumenical Bishop who would give oversight to the Local Ecumenical Projects. Both of these are examples of emerging patterns of personal forms of ecumenical oversight.

The shared oversight exercised by the Sponsoring Bodies is closely related to the sharing together of those who have a ministry of oversight in a locality – the United Reformed Church Moderator, the Methodist Chairman of District, the Baptist Superintendent and the Anglican and Roman Catholic Bishops. Formal covenants describe the tasks and extent of shared oversight and the degree of mutual accountability. This might be described as a form of ecumenical collegiality. It is a way by which those who exercise a ministry of oversight in one tradition learn what that ministry entails in another tradition. In two places in England regional ecumenical councils are an additional form of shared oversight.

* * *

These new and developing forms of shared oversight show characteristics that can be described as personal, collegial and communal. They testify to a desire on the part of local Christians to live a united life and the recognized need for the local Christian community to be served by a ministry of oversight which represents the wider reality of the church's life – a ministry which keeps the local community connected to the "wider fellowship of the church". However, they also raise questions and concerns:

– Is there a danger that churches within an LEP might experience a weakened sense of belonging to a Christian World Communion? Is it possible that an LEP might tend towards isolation, or even towards forming a new denomination?

– Does the sharing of the eucharist in LEPs, and the different interpretations which the participating churches place on this sharing, obscure the integral relation between the eucharist and the ministry?

– It is not always clear in an LEP who ensures both functionally and symbolically the continuity of the faith of the church through the ages. The very "localness" of the LEP needs to be balanced by a sense of continuity.

– The integral relation between the totality of the life of the church, held in the continuity of faith, sacraments, ministry and conciliar life, might be called into question by these new forms of local Christian life unless they are conscious of the continuing relationship to the wider life of all the participating churches.

– There is an added burden on the Ecumenical Moderator (and will be on the Ecumenical Bishop), who must remain in contact with the structures of oversight in all of the participating churches.

While these issues are indeed problematic for some of us – as for some of the churches involved in LEPs – we all recognize the desire for greater unity and more effective mission that motivates these new developments. We also recognize that the setting up of an Ecumenical Moderator and the proposal for an Ecumenical Bishop represent a recognition by all the participating churches of the need for a personal exercise of oversight in the local Christian community. Moreover, the covenanted sharing of those with a ministry of oversight in the participating churches points to the ministry of collegiality in the exercise of oversight. This sharing gives those from episcopal and non-episcopal churches the opportunity to experience directly the values of their different traditions. And the emergence of ecumenical councils at regional levels points to the bringing together of ordained and lay, with those who are entrusted with personal oversight, for a "communal" experience of oversight. In these ways the theological convergence noted in *BEM* is being affirmed in the lived experience of the local churches.

3. Ecumenical developments and proposals, national and regional

In many parts of the world, certain churches are involved in union agreements at various stages of development. Participants in this consultation were able on the basis of first-hand experience to describe the history and current status of several church union agreements which have been achieved or were, at the time of the meeting, in the process of negotiation. Each agreement process has needed to address the issue of oversight in its own way, and several in particular have elicited reflections and questions for further consideration.

a. The Church Unity Commission (CUC), South Africa

The Church Unity Commission in South Africa comprises six churches in the Anglican, Congregational, Methodist and Presbyterian traditions. It was formed in 1968. In 1974 its member churches accepted a "Declaration of Intention to Seek Union" in which they indicated that each of them belonged to the one local church of God and was linked with the church of apostolic times by a continuity of faith and common allegiance to Jesus Christ. They recognized each other's ministries as real and effective, accepted the sacraments of baptism and holy communion in each church and agreed to admit to holy communion the baptized and communicant members of other member churches. In 1989 the Church of the Province of Southern Africa (Anglican) agreed to accept through transfer, without further sacramental rite, communicant members of the other churches who had been baptized and made profession of faith.

Church union concerns were not considered important during the struggle against apartheid after 1976. The situation changed in the 1990s. On the one hand, the removal of the common enemy undermined the ecumenical solidarity of the struggle, and churches tended to lapse into denominational isolation. On the other hand, it was recognized that the church could not credibly call for reconciliation when it was not itself reconciled.

In March 1993, a meeting of Anglican and Methodist bishops with the executives of the Congregational and Presbyterian churches instructed the Church Unity Commission to prepare proposals for the recognition and reconciliation of the ordained ministries of its member churches. In response the Commission proposed a two-stage process.

In the first stage member churches were asked to accept "that the ordained ministers of Word and Sacrament in the member churches of the CUC have been called and ordained by God in Christ through his church and exercise a sacramental, preaching, teaching and pastoral ministry in the church of God and not simply in the particular church to which they belong". They were further asked to permit these ministers to officiate in the other churches while remaining ministers within their own church "when duly authorized or appointed so to do". Ministers who wished to transfer from one church to another would have to follow the procedures laid down by the receiving church. In the case of the Church of the Province of Southern Africa this would necessitate episcopal ordination. The second stage would involve a search for consensus on the ministry of oversight which would open the way to full reconciliation of the ordained ministries.

The two-stage process was proposed because previous attempts to effect reconciliation in one step had failed, due to the perception that the acceptance of non-episcopal ministries depended upon the acceptance of episcopacy, thus casting doubts upon the ordination of such ministers. The limited acceptance involved in the first stage made it clear that this was not the case. It was believed that this would allow the ministry of oversight to be discussed in a less emotionally charged atmosphere. This disappointed some in the non-episcopal churches but made it possible for the Anglicans to take an important step forward.

Stage one was accepted by all member churches during 1995, opening the way to closer co-operation in ministry and mission at the local level. While there have not yet been any cross-denominational appointments, the position of ministers in united congregations has been regularized. Reception will obviously take time and will proceed at different paces in different places.

The CUC is now engaged in a process of consultation on the ministry of oversight. Local consultations have been held in several areas, and their reports will be laid before the Commission. The member churches will be asked to examine their own exercise of *episkopé* to see whether changes can be made that will enable each church to recognize in the others those factors of *episkopé* which it considers needful for full reconciliation of the ordained ministries. As organic union is not an immediate objective, it will not be necessary for the pattern of oversight to be identical. If reconciliation can be achieved, the churches will be asked to move forward into a relationship of conciliarity as a further step on the way to visible unity.

Reflections and Questions
– Fundamental to the understanding of this agreement are the notion of gradual steps and stages on the way to visible unity and the demand of mission and witness in the particular context of Southern Africa.
– What is this agreement saying to other churches in other places about the imperative to unity?
– Is there a common understanding of the sort of united life of the church, the visible *koinonia*, to which this is leading? Or will this emerge as the process continues?
– What changes and renewal in the exercise of a ministry of oversight will happen as a result of the shared life of the participating churches? And what form or forms of *episkopé* will develop as these churches grow together?
– The new situation provides a renewed context for facing issues of the personal exercise of *episkopé*. Already changes are taking place internally in the life of the churches.

b. The Meissen Agreement between the Church of England and the Evangelical Church in Germany (EKD)
On a visit to Germany in 1993, Archbishop of Canterbury Robert Runcie proposed that closer relations be established between the Church of England and the churches of what was at that time a divided Germany. Conversations began in 1985 – with all the difficulties entailed by the division of the German churches on the two sides of the Wall.

Published in 1988, the report of the conversations, *On the Way to Visible Unity*, sets out a common understanding of the visible unity of the church to which the partners are committed. This portrait owes much to the description offered at the WCC's sixth assembly (Vancouver 1983): a common confession of the apostolic faith in word and life, the sharing of one baptism, the celebration of one eucharist and the service of a reconciled common ministry.

Integral to the Meissen Agreement is a consensus that the full visible unity of the church entails a ministry of oversight *at every level of the church's life*. A united life together will entail bonds of communion which will enable the church at every level to guard and interpret the apostolic faith, to take decisions, to teach authoritatively, to share goods and to bear effective witness in the world. These bonds of communion will take personal, collegial and communal forms. At every level they are outward and visible signs of the communion between persons, who through their baptism and eucharistic fellowship are drawn into the fellowship of the Triune God. Here the Report is influenced by the convergence of the *BEM* document.

The *Meissen Common Statement* lists the agreements in faith which the churches already share, harvesting the work of international bilateral and multilateral dialogues rather than repeating the theological work so recently done by the churches. (One consequence of the use of international theological documents is that a consistency is maintained between regional developments and the position of the world communions of the participating churches.) The report is honest about where difference still remains: Lutherans, Reformed and United churches, though increasingly prepared to appreciate episcopal succession "as a sign of apostolicity of the life of the whole church, hold that this particular form of *episkopé* should not become a necessary condition for full visible unity". The Anglican understanding of full visible unity, on the other hand, includes the historic episcopal succession with the full interchangeability of ministers (para. 16).

On the basis of the agreed portrait of full visible unity, stated agreements in faith and an honest recognition of the outstanding differences on *episkopé,* apostolicity and succession, the churches involved signed a formal Declaration in 1992 committing themselves to a greater degree of shared living appropriate to the extent of agreement in faith recorded and to the close relationship which had existed over many years. In this Declaration the churches made mutual acknowledgments:
– of one another's churches as churches belonging to the one holy, catholic and apostolic church of Jesus Christ and truly participating in the apostolic mission;
– of each other as churches in which the Word of God is authentically preached and the sacraments are duly administered;
– of each other's ordained ministries as given by God and instruments of God's grace.

For Anglicans the official acknowledgment (or recognition) of the ordained ministry of the Evangelical Church in Germany marks a significant stage on the way to visible unity. It does not however imply an interchangeability of ministries or what Anglicans would describe as the "reconciliation of ministries". Beyond the recognition of authentic ministries in other churches lies the bringing together of separated ministries within the bringing together of the lives of communities – in other words, the reconciliation of ministries as an integral part of the reconciliation of churches. This greater unity is to be signified in a single ministry in the historic episcopal succession, within a single collegial and conciliar life of the churches.

Even so, the churches do make binding commitments to one another in the formal Declaration. These commitments are to work at outstanding differences to establish new forms of joint oversight which will maintain the new relationships, to encourage exchanges and twinnings, and to receive the eucharist in each other's churches. Clergy are encouraged to share together in the celebration of the eucharist – not in place of one another nor concelebration – but in a way that visibly testifies to the closeness of the churches and beckons them to move towards a single interchangeable ministry and life.

The Meissen Commission, set up to give joint oversight to the developing relationship between the partner churches, has been instrumental in the last five years in holding the churches accountable to the commitments they made in 1992. Theological discussions have begun to explore the remaining outstanding issues of *episkopé* and episcopacy, apostolicity and succession.[1] They have also identified the need to discuss further the understandings (and misunderstandings) of the terms "recognition" and "reconciliation" as these are used in relation to the ministry.

Reflections
– It is necessary to clarify what is meant by "recognition" and "reconciliation" in the *Meissen Common Statement* and how this relates to the different stages of relationship envisaged in the Lutheran-Episcopal Concordat (USA) and the COCU proposals (USA), as well as to "acceptance" as used in the Southern African proposal.
– Is there a consistency between what is agreed about a ministry of *episkopé* and episcopacy in the Meissen Agreement and in the Concordat (cf. below)? Is there a consistency between Meissen and the Lutheran-Reformed dialogue in the USA?
– How far have the structures of oversight established as a result of Meissen encouraged the development of a closer fellowship?
– What progress has been made on the outstanding issues of *episkopé* and episcopacy, apostolicity and succession as a result of this agreement? Are the participating churches any nearer to reaching agreement as a result of their experience and theological dialogue?

c. The Porvoo Agreement between the Anglican churches of Britain and Ireland and Nordic and Baltic Lutheran churches
Between 1909 and 1951 theological conversations between Anglicans and Lutherans led to a number of piecemeal agreements between the Church of England and some of the Nordic and Baltic Lutheran churches. In 1988 Archbishop Robert Runcie suggested that it was now time to look at these several agreements in the light of more recent theological conversations to see whether Lutheran and Anglican churches in Europe could move to greater visible unity. When conversations began in 1989, momentous changes were taking place in Europe, giving the sense that this was a *kairos* moment for the unity of churches in northern Europe. The missionary imperative was a dominant and controlling impulse throughout the talks.

The Anglican churches of Britain and Ireland and the Nordic and Baltic Lutheran churches are all episcopal churches. Most of them have bishops consecrated in the historic episcopal succession, although the Church of Denmark was forced at the Reformation to maintain a presbyteral succession but subsequently returned to episcopal consecrations.

The report of the conversations, published in 1993, follows the same simple logic and dynamic as the *Meissen Common Statement*. Having affirmed the imperative for shared mission in the new European context brought about by the fall of communism, the report sets out a common understanding of the nature and unity of the church and a portrait of the kind of visibly united church, with diversity, which Anglicans and Lutherans are committed to becoming together. The portrait of unity is very close to that in the *Meissen Common Statement* and rests upon the same multilateral statements of the World Council of Churches and the results of bilateral dialogues. Next comes a series of 12 agreements in faith, like Meissen harvesting the fruits of bilateral and multilateral conversations. Unlike Meissen, there was no need in the Porvoo document to record differences on the understandings of *episkopé* and episcopacy, apostolicity and succession. Instead there is a lengthy agreed theological statement on episcopacy in the service of the apostolicity of the church.[2] The agreement is based upon a common understanding of the apostolicity of the whole church, *episkopé* and episcopacy in the service of the apostolicity of the whole church, the episcopal office in the service of the apostolic succession and the historic episcopal succession as sign, which the text describes as "effective sign":

> The use of the sign of the historic episcopal succession does not by itself guarantee the fidelity of a church to every aspect of the apostolic faith, life and mission... Nonetheless, the retention of the sign remains a permanent challenge to fidelity and to unity, a summons to witness to, and a commission to realize more fully, the permanent characteristics of the church of the apostles (para. 51).

The theological agreements led the Anglican churches of Britain and Ireland and the Nordic and Baltic Lutheran churches (except Latvia, which has not yet voted, and Denmark, which has abstained from signing the Agreement) to ratify a Common Declaration. Because this agreement includes the establishment of a reconciled ministry in the historic episcopal succession, it has implications for the conciliar life of the Anglican communion. The *Porvoo Common Statement* was thus sent to the Meeting of Anglican primates, who invited comments from all of the provinces of the Anglican communion. The responses received were presented to the General Synod of the Church of England when it came to take its decision.

The churches signing the Porvoo Declaration acknowledge each other as belonging to the one holy, catholic and apostolic church, as churches in which the word of God is authentically preached and the sacraments duly administered. There is an acknowledgment that each other's ministries are given by God and that in them the episcopal office is valued and maintained as a visible sign expressing the church's unity and continuity. On the basis of these acknowledgments a number of commitments are made: to share a common life and mission, to regard baptized members of all the churches as members of each church, to welcome ministers episcopally ordained to serve by invitation, to invite bishops to take part in the ordination of bishops and to set up forms of collegial and conciliar consultation.

The coming into being of the Porvoo Communion of churches was celebrated in Norway, Estonia and London in 1996. A contact group was established to oversee the developing relations and to set up a meeting of church leaders to explore common challenges. The primates of the participating churches met in Norway, and the Archbishop of Canterbury invited them to attend the Lambeth Conference.

The Porvoo Agreement has brought these churches into a communion of faith, sacraments, ministry and bonded life in the service of the witness and mission of the church in northern Europe. A regular ministry of oversight is integral to the new relationship, as is the establishment of collegial and communal forms of the exercise of oversight.

Reflections

The Porvoo Agreement raises the following issues regarding the ministry of oversight:

- What effect does the new Porvoo Communion have upon relations with and between the two world communions involved?
- What are the implications of Porvoo for the relation between the Nordic and Baltic Lutheran churches and other Lutheran churches in Europe and elsewhere? Similarly, what are its implications for other churches of the Anglican communion?
- What does the agreement on *episkopé*, apostolicity and succession imply for other agreements?
- Will such agreements, while strengthening regional unity and a regional exercise of *episkopé* and episcopacy, lead to the establishment of a communion "beyond" the Anglican communion? Does the strengthening of a ministry of *episkopé* at the regional level in the service of *koinonia* damage the *koinonia* of the church at world level?
- What does the Porvoo Agreement reveal about the bonds of *episkopé* which exist in the Anglican communion or the Lutheran World Federation?

d. The Leuenberg Agreement, Europe

The Leuenberg Agreement of 1973 established full church fellowship among Lutheran and Reformed churches in Europe, the United churches which grew out of them, and the related pre-Reformation churches (the Waldensian Church and the Church of the Czech Brethren), on the basis of an elaboration of a common understanding of the gospel. In February 1997 the Fellowship was extended to include the Methodist churches of Europe.

A key statement in the Leuenberg Agreement is that "in the view of the Reformation it follows that agreement in the right teaching of the gospel and in the right administration of the sacraments is *the necessary and sufficient prerequisite for the true unity of the church*" (para. 2). In consequence, "the practice and form of the church should be determined only by the commission to deliver this testimony to the world, and the Word of God remains sovereign over every human ordering of the Christian community" (para. 4).

While acknowledging that considerable differences remain in forms of worship, types of spirituality and church order, "the signatory churches accord each other *the freedom to promote intercelebration (die Ermöglichung der Interzelebration)*" (para. 28). Thus mutual recognition does not exhaust the matter. It opens the way for but does not of itself complete the provision for intercelebration and revision of "the rules in force in the participating churches for induction to a pastoral charge, the exercise of the pastoral ministry or the ordering of congregational life" (para. 43). The rules remain and need to be deliberately changed before full exchange of ministries operates between any two of the signatory churches or any group of churches.

While the Leuenberg Agreement does not commit its signatory churches to a binding common *episkopé* or a common ordering of *episkopé*, it does commit them "to strive for the fullest possible cooperation in witness and service to the world" (para. 29). In pursuit of this common witness, plenary assemblies of the churches have been regularly held, and an Executive Committee meets every two years. On at least one occasion, the Executive Committee has commented on a potentially problematic action by a member church and convinced it to modify its course.

Much of the reflection on ecclesiology, ministry and *episkopé* which has gone on in the Leuenberg Church Fellowship is summarized in the text, *The Church of Jesus Christ*, accepted by its general assembly in Vienna in May 1994. This text repeats the statements on *episkopé* in the Tampere Theses on *The Discussion of the Ministry Today*:

> The Lutheran as well as the Reformed and the United churches recognize pastoral care and *episkopé* as belonging to the ordained ministry both in the individual congregation and also at a level (regional and beyond that, national) going beyond the congregation. Nevertheless..., proclamation of the gospel is the obligation for the whole congregation and the leadership of the congregation is also exercised through other ministries and does not only fall to the ordained ministry... Although the churches participating in the Leuenberg Agreement have come from their historically conditioned traditions with differing structures of church leadership, they are nevertheless agreed that such differences in church structures do not impede a "church fellowship" in the sense of pulpit and altar fellowship... They also recognize that in the wider ecumenical discussion they can and should learn from other non-Reformation churches, but they hold that no single historically arisen form of church leadership and ministerial structure can or may be laid down as a prior condition for fellowship and for mutual recognition.

e. Consultation on Church Union (COCU), United States of America

The Consultation on Church Union, an ecumenical effort among nine communions in the USA, has worked since 1960 to establish a church "truly Catholic, truly Reformed and truly Evangelical" which finds unity in "sacred things" – faith, sacraments, ministry and mission. Through recognized and reconciled ministries, the hope is that "one may be able to exercise ministry on behalf of all" at different levels of the church's life.

The ministry of *episkopé* in the Church of Christ Uniting is to be located within the ordinary structures (presbyteries, conferences, dioceses, etc.) of each communion, and in local, regional and national Covenanting Councils. The task of a Covenanting Council to ensure that the covenant of agreement with and among the nine communions is honoured and lived into.

In the covenantal agreement each communion promises to identify and put forward persons, both women and men, who will exercise *episkopé* in concert with others. *Episkopé* is identified in the covenant as being but one manifestation of an ordained vocation. It grows out of a theology of baptism in which the ministry of all the baptized is primary, and from this primary ministry a few are called and set apart for oversight.

Within the Covenant, *episkopé* is identified as personal, collegial and communal. It is always grounded in the ministry of the whole people of God and never to be exercised monarchically or exclusively. Ministers of oversight, called bishops by some within the COCU communion, gather in regional Covenanting Councils to shepherd the work of local Covenanting Councils. Ordinations in the various communions are overseen by regional Covenanting Councils, which also deploy ministers of oversight – bishops – to ordain.

The ministry of oversight is marked by nine "episcopal" characteristics. A minister of oversight is to be (1) a liturgical leader, (2) ordinarily presiding in sacramental liturgies, (3) a teacher of the apostolic faith, (4) a pastoral overseer, (5) a leader in mission, (6) a minister in the act of ordination, (7) an administrative leader, (8) a servant of unity, and (9) a participant in governance.

Recognition and reconciliation of ministries within one Church of Christ Uniting takes place in a series of covenanting liturgies, nationally, regionally and locally. Within the liturgies ministers and ministries are reconciled through the laying-on of hands, in silence, an act which is intended to convey reconciliation and blessing, but *not* re-ordination.

The proposal for a Church of Christ Uniting has encountered significant resistance from two sources. First, the Episcopal Church, while having participated in the drafting of *The COCU Consensus* and *Church in Covenant Communion*, has been unable finally to affirm that the COCU model of *episkopé* is consistent with the final point of the Chicago-Lambeth Quadrilateral – the historic episcopate, locally adapted. More recently, however, developments in the process towards a Concordat of Agreement between the Evangelical Lutheran Church and the Episcopal Church have given Episcopal ecumenical leaders a new perspective on the COCU proposal. Not placing episcopal leadership (*episkopé*) on the level of the gospel and temporarily suspending the Ordinal in the *Book of Common Prayer* (as in the Concordat process) may also enable the Episcopal Church to embrace more fully the COCU proposal.

Second, a proposal before the General Assembly of the Presbyterian Church in which *episkopé* would be exercised by a minister of Word and Sacrament – to be called Presbytery Bishop – in conjunction with an ordained elder was not well received. Some Presbyterians feared that an episcopal office, or indeed the word "bishop", would undermine the integrity of the Presbyterian system. Others feared the possibility of the "creeping power of a monarchical episcopate". After debate, a modified proposal was put forward, suggesting that the Presbyterian Church create a commission to represent a presbytery when a minister of oversight was required. The commission would be composed of equal numbers of ministers and elders. As this report is being drafted, the modified proposal is before the Presbyterian Church for a vote, and approval looks unlikely.

To find a way forward, the COCU Executive Committee has called together a Commission composed of theologians from the nine churches. Their charge is to assess the responses of the nine churches and to recommend any action which could be taken at the next Plenary of the Consultation. While it is impossible at this writing to predict the outcome of their work, two themes emerged from their initial conversation: (1) that COCU should ensure that all nine member communions were included in any next steps; and (2) that the most helpful way forward might be found in identifying, claiming and affirming the parts of the proposal upon which all can now agree.

f. The Concordat of Agreement, United States of America

Episcopalians and Lutherans in the United States began their most recent series of dialogues in the late 1960s. These dialogues quickly identified large areas of consensus and urged their sponsoring churches to move towards a relationship of full communion. In 1982 the Lutheran-Episcopal Agreement, approved by three Lutheran churches and the Episcopal Church, stated that the goal of Lutheran-Episcopal dialogue was full communion. The churches involved in the dialogue recognized each other as churches in which the gospel is proclaimed, encouraged joint mission and study and entered into an "interim sharing of the eucharist".

A third series of dialogues was established in order to provide greater assurance that the sponsoring churches indeed proclaimed the same gospel and had a common understanding and means to arrive at a common ministry. The final series of dialogues produced two reports: *Implications of the Gospel* addressed the initial part of the mandate; and *The Concordat of Agreement* took up questions of ministry, especially episcopal ministry, which has long been a stumbling block in Anglican-Lutheran relations.

This latter document must be considered in the total context of the dialogue and its specific mandate. Based on a consensus on the gospel (cf. *Implications of the Gospel)* and agreement in faith, the Concordat was designed to challenge the churches to move beyond the agreement of 1982 and into a relationship of full communion with full recognition and exchangeability of ordained ministries. Some described this text as an ecumenical breakthrough. For the sake of full communion, Episcopalians would agree for the first time to a temporary suspension of the requirement of episcopal ordination contained in the preface to the 17th-century Ordinal in the *Book of Common Prayer*. To the same end, Lutherans would accept the elimination of required subscription to the Lutheran confession from a non-Lutheran church.

The Concordat provided a basis for both churches to take unparalleled actions so that each could accept the claims of the other. Both were freed from questions of validity and certain aspects of conditionality, and could thus enter into a process placing them in full communion. A major motivation for this agreement with its specific characteristic was the possibility of enhancing the mission of both churches. The Concordat offered the possibility for an episcopally ordered church and a non-episcopally ordered church to enter into a more complete model of visible unity while remaining constant with their own tradition. The Concordat will be voted upon by the Episcopal Church in the USA and the Evangelical Lutheran Church in America in the summer of 1997.

Some concluding reflections

Overall, this survey of developments in the exercise of the ministry of *episkopé* at local, national and regional levels in different parts of the world raises some issues and questions which need to be addressed in the interest of coherence and consistency in the development of oversight:

– What are the implications of these developments for our understanding of the structures of oversight in the church, on the personal, collegial and communal levels?
– What are the features of the shared oversight described in some of these situations and developments? How does this relate to the ongoing exercise of oversight in the

participating churches? What are its implications for developing a common understanding of the structures of oversight that would hold us in full visible unity?

- To what explicit or implicit portrait of visible unity are these developments leading? How do the developing forms of oversight relate to the forms of oversight that would serve visible communion?
- Is a common understanding emerging on the relationship between the ministry of oversight in the church and the common faith and the sacramental life of the church?
- Do the developments described involve anomalies (for example, in the suspension of church discipline) which may be tolerated for the sake of movement towards visible unity? Are these tolerable not only for the partners involved but also for other sister churches and/or ecumenical partners?
- What do these developments say about the functions of *episkopé*: leadership in mission, teaching of the faith, the care for unity and focus of unity, the care for continuity and focus of continuity?
- What is the responsibility of each world communion for maintaining and nurturing developments in different parts of its communion? How are co-ordination and accountability to be ensured between the developments in different world communions?
- How are technical terms such as "full communion", "organic union", "recognition", "reconciliation" and "acceptance" being used in these particular developments? How can we be helped to move towards a common understanding of these terms?

This developing experience of a ministry of oversight, both within and between churches, sheds light on the paragraphs in *BEM* about the personal, collegial and communal forms of oversight at the different levels of the church's life. A ministry of oversight belongs to the life of the whole church, in which those set apart for an ordered ministry work in, with and among the *laos*, the whole people of God, and in a proper and inter-related sense are together the *laos*. With the help of a ministry of oversight the community is held together in its fidelity to the apostolic faith and strengthened for mission and service.

The emergence of a ministry of *shared* oversight is an important stage on the way to visible unity, a foretaste of that single ministry of oversight which belongs to visible unity.

It is in the context of a recognition of the ministry of oversight which exists in all churches, episcopal and non-episcopal, and the developing experience of shared oversight that the theological issues raised by the present consultations on *episkopé* and episcopacy are addressed.

NOTES

[1] *Visible Unity and the Ministry of Oversight,* Report of the Second Theological Conference held under the Meissen Agreement, London, Church House Publishing, 1997.

[2] Cf. *Apostolicity and Succession*, Occasional Paper of the House of Bishops of the Church of England, London, 1994.

PRELIMINARY THEOLOGICAL REFLECTIONS

Report of Group II

Introduction

Before addressing the theological issues surrounding the exercise of *episkopé*, it is useful to set out the context, both past and present, out of which these issues arise. This group reflected on the historical legacy which has led to current conceptions and practices of oversight, contemporary opportunities for a way forward and the matter of power – its uses and abuses – in ecclesiastical oversight.

All our churches agree on the *need* for *episkopé*, the content of which is understood to be care for unity, truth, nurture and growth (cf. Eph. 4). All our churches provide in some form or other for this task, to be undertaken by persons or groups of persons. The issue is, what form or forms shall *episkopé* take? We do not come to this discussion with a *tabula rasa* but out of historical contexts which may be described – all too briefly – as follows.

Historical perspectives

As was already expressed and widely agreed in *BEM*,

> the New Testament does not describe a single pattern of ministry which might serve as a blueprint or continuing norm for all future ministry in the church. In the New Testament there appears rather a variety of forms which existed at different places and times. As the Holy Spirit continued to lead the church in life, worship and mission, certain elements from this early variety were further developed and became settled into a more universal pattern of ministry (Ministry, para. 19).

Scripture and tradition together are the basis for this pattern. For example, St Ignatius of Antioch writes:

All of you follow the bishop, as Jesus Christ followed the Father, and the presbytery as the Apostles; respect the deacons as the ordinance of God... Wherever the bishop shall appear, there let the people be; just as wherever Christ Jesus may be, there is the catholic church (*Smyrn.* 8, i-ii; cf. also *Trall.* 3, i; *Magn.* 6, i).

Although *BEM* spoke of this as a "threefold pattern", in the Western church at least that phrase is an over-simplification of the historical development.

Following the era of the Apostolic Fathers, the interdependence of ministries continued, despite uncertainty in some churches regarding a clear and final distinction between bishop and presbyter (for example in Alexandria, as evident in the writings of St Jerome). However, a clear and normative pattern of sacramental *episkopé* exercised by the bishop emerged and prevailed in most areas of the church within the early centuries. According to an interpretation of this pattern, the bishop is the *ikon* and sacramental presence of Christ; he presides over the one baptism and one eucharist of the church; he exercises a *charisma veritatis* and is the guardian of truth; he passes on the ministries of the church as an expression of its *episkopé* and safeguards its apostolicity. The bishop represents the church and serves its unity, both synchronically and diachronically.

At the Reformation, which is here seen as the outcome of a long period of stresses and strains in church life, the leaders of some Christian communities felt constrained to seek renewal by a return to what they believed to be the primitive pattern of church life and ministry. In part they did this as a deliberately emergency action, regretting any loss of continuity with episcopal order; in part they chose to revert to an order in which "*presbyteroi/episkopoi*" – in the manner of the Pauline churches – exercised a conciliar leadership.

After the Reformation and in the modern period of missionary outreach around the world, both the traditional ministerial pattern and those forms developed at the Reformation and subsequently produced new and fruitful expressions of Christian community, as well as denominational conflicts which scandalized new Christians. A vital part of the modern ecumenical responsibility of the churches has thus been to seek a renewal of ministry under the guidance of the Holy Spirit. Valued elements in this renewal have come both from ancient tradition and from contemporary responses to new situations. The questions about ministry before this consultation are not juridical questions about outward forms and order but ask how the church of Jesus Christ can be obedient in ministry, "personal, collegial and communal".

Present realities and opportunities

The renewed willingness today to engage this question for the sake of the mission, unity and wholeness of the church is characterized by:
– a letting go of the excluding judgments of the past;
– an openness to the guidance of the Holy Spirit for the future;
– a willingness to share inheritances;
– a capacity to acknowledge deformations and bad examples from the past and in the present;
– new insights into the corporate reality of the life of the church, constituting a "common life/*koinonia*" through the redeeming blood of Christ (1 John 1);
– an understanding of the church as an eschatological sign of the kingdom of God.

We further agree that it is helpful to understand the exercise of *episkopé* as personal, collegial (or in solidarity) and communal, as affirmed in the Ministry section of *BEM* (para. 26). This structure helps us to see both the commonality in the practice of *episkopé* and those points at which practice is open to transformation (reform and renewal).

We understand that there may well be differences in the balance between these ways of exercising *episkopé*, which may correspond to differences of historical experience and social and political culture. But it is legitimate to ask how the unity, truth and nurture of the whole church is served by these differences.

Clarification is also needed in relation to the "personal" dimension of *episkopé*. According to the *BEM* paragraph cited above, the exercise of ordained ministry

> should be *personal* because the presence of Christ among his people can most effectively be pointed to by the person ordained to proclaim the gospel and to call the community to serve the Lord in unity of life and witness.

We note the term "pointed to". There is indeed only one Chief Shepherd, Jesus Christ. The "elders" of the community are shepherds together with him and exercise their role of oversight in relation to him (1 Pet. 5).

BEM sets its entire treatment of the ordained ministry within the context of the calling of the whole people of God, upon whom the Holy Spirit bestows "diverse and complementary gifts" (Ministry, para. 5). "Through baptism Christians are brought into union with Christ, with each other and with the church of every time and place" (Baptism, para. 6). Baptism involves a consecration to mission and service as a living member of the body of Christ.

The calling of an ordained minister, both a priest/presbyter and an *episkopos,* is a calling to service and responsibility within the body of Christ. In ordination the church prays for and the Holy Spirit bestows a gift from God for the specific offices and work of ministry, through the laying on of hands (2 Tim. 1:6). It should never be a cause for spiritual pride or a feeling of superiority. In the kingdom of God it is the least who is the greatest (Luke 9:48). Ordained ministers are "bound to the faithful in interdependence and reciprocity" (Ministry, para. 16). Within the interdependence and reciprocity of the gifts of the Spirit which make the life of the Body of Christ is a specific gift related to a specific way of exercising ministry (*diakonia*) for the good of the whole *koinonia* as such.

This gift is exercised in differing but not necessarily mutually incompatible ways in different churches. Some churches distribute *episkopé* among a variety of people or groups. They do so in a deliberate and ordered way, intending to make clear the unique headship of Christ over his church and to avoid the temptations to which the personal office of *episkopos* is open. Other churches directly identify bishops as such by ordination. They invoke the assistance of the Holy Spirit for discharging the responsibilities and resisting the temptations of the office. In all cases bishops are charged to work co-operatively with fellow ministers and the people (Ministry, para. 15).

There is here a marked coincidence of intent in teaching. In the theology of the *episkopos,* bishops are said to be *ikons* or images of Christ, acting *in persona Christi.* They are images not only of the glorified Lord, but of Christ the servant, who set his disciples an example by washing their feet (John 13:14-15). As sinful human beings they are dependent upon the grace of Christ, through the power of the Holy Spirit. Bishops receive the anointing of the same Spirit who animates the life of all believers and are inseparably bound to them. The intent of this teaching is that bishops should not be exalted above the community and should point to the unique mediatorial work of Christ, not to themselves. The temptation to self-exaltation is classically acknowledged (for example by St John Chrysostom and by Gregory the Great). It is admitted with sorrow that the office has been seriously distorted by confusion with political power or social status, and by the actions of those who have exercised it despotically. It should be possible to remove from office bishops who become scandals to their calling.

It has proved more difficult to reach a common mind on whether it is preferable for the personal office of *episkopé* to be held by a publicly named and identified individual or by a variable group. The former is the tradition of episcopal churches, and it is claimed that it was so intended by Christ and his apostles. Both in the 16th century and in the historical-critical movement these claims have been challenged; and the dispute has not been resolved to the satisfaction of all. It is said that there are advantages to the church when specific persons commit themselves to a lifelong, "identity-constituting" role, and grow in confidence and competence in their tasks. Such claims are of their nature contingent and historical, and lend themselves to being undermined by contrary experience (for example, of bishops who have grown proud and remote from their people). But perhaps all could acknowledge that the early development of all named ordained ministries occurred under the general guidance of the Holy Spirit, and that they were from the very first days attended by disadvantages and temptations. This would affirm and value the testimonies of both those who have persisted with the tradition of named bishops and on biblical grounds receive the office as a gift, not a burden, and of those who, also on biblical grounds, have warned against its dangers.

Among the principal tasks of the *episkopoi* is to ordain and send priests to share with them in Christ's mission through the ministry of word and sacrament in a specific locality. These tasks, together with that of discipline, are a central way in which they exercise their care for the unity, faithfulness in truth and nurture of the people of God. In churches which do not have named bishops these tasks are likewise carried out by persons bearing responsibility for *episkopé* with seriousness and care. In all cases the intention is reverently to esteem and to continue the office given by Christ to his church, through prayer to the Holy Spirit and the laying on of hands. It is an act performed only by those specially authorized so to do. In all cases the congregations are explicitly involved and invited to consent to the act and to join in prayer for the candidates.

Some remarks about power

We study this subject for two main reasons:
- It figures prominently in the confessional documents of some of the churches of the Reformation, especially in relation to the person of the bishop (for example, Article 28 of the Augsburg Confession).
- There is intense consciousness of the abuse of power by 20th-century political dictators, and consequently a concern about checks and balances on and accountability for the exercise of power within the church.

What power or powers properly belong to the church both in its own government and in its relation to civil power?

We are clear that there is a sense of the word "power" (Greek, *dynamis, exousia,* sometimes interchangeable, sometimes stressing the power itself, or the mode of its exercise) which is wholly positive and constructive. The vast resources of God's power are open to us who have faith, and this power is the same as that which was at work in Christ's resurrection (Eph. 1:19-20). The gospel is the saving power of God for everyone who has faith (Rom. 1:15). The disciples wait to be armed with "power from above", the gift of the Holy Spirit (Luke 24:39; Acts 1:8). Through this power the witness of the church takes place with boldness and conviction. The apostle Paul, though acutely feeling his own weakness, nevertheless speaks the word of truth powerfully and wants to use his authority constructively to build up his quarrelling congregation (2 Cor. 13).

But this is power of a very particular kind. Like the power of the Lord himself, it is for announcing good news to the poor, for releasing prisoners, for healing, for proclaiming the kingdom (Luke 4:18). It is vulnerable power, which refuses the sword and legions of angels (Matt. 26:52). It is a power to lay down one's life (John 10:18), which persists until the great work of redemption is finished (John 19:30). It is a power which reverses the order of the world, putting down the mighty and raising up the humble (Luke 1:52). It is a power by which Jesus Christ, *because* he humbled himself and·was obedient to death, was exalted and given the name above every name (Phil. 2:5-11). The power of the transcendent God, and therefore the work of every form of divine power in the church, takes the way of the cross and lives under its sign.

From the beginning the disciples of Jesus found this teaching bewildering and difficult to implement. At the Last Supper itself, according to Luke's account, a dispute arose over which of them should be considered greatest (Luke 22:24). Jesus' statement, "I am with you like a servant" (Luke 22:27), and his example of washing his disciples' feet (John 13:2-17) permanently challenge the church in every age to interrogate its own uses of power, lest the love of money and strategies of domination intrude upon its performance of the tasks of leadership (1 Pet. 5:1-4).

We agree that the exercise of power of various kinds is literally unavoidable in the daily life of the church. The first step towards a scrutiny of how power is used is an honest recognition that this is so. Law is part of the ordering of all our churches. It may on occasion involve coercion, that is, be enforceable (for example, in relation to qualification for office and in relation to discipline). In all these cases rules of natural justice need to be followed, including the right of appeal.

But each Christian has at his or her disposal power of various kinds to build up or pull down the body of Christ. Although baptism confers a unique and equal status in God's sight on every baptized person, inequality of access to the capacity to influence the life of the church is a feature of all our churches. For example, election or appointment to a decision-making assembly gives some persons a greater opportunity to exercise power in the church than others. For power to be exercised responsibly and in the fear of God, this inequality must be recognized, not concealed or denied. It is part of the essential work of *episkopé* that those with greater opportunities should themselves be committed to an open process of teaching and learning by which the conscience of the whole people of God is informed and built up. Such activity is an empowering of the discernment of those who have less access to the decision-making process, but who are an integral part of the right judging of matters of faith and life.

There is a practical wisdom or skill, a "sanctified common sense", in the use of power, arising from an understanding of and concern for the whole people of God. The church recognizes gifts of wisdom in certain people, and sets them apart for ministries of oversight, praying that God will enlighten them, give them insight and protect them from temptation.

Much experience in the life of the church suggests that it is prudent that there should be opportunities – such as pastoral conferences, synods and other assemblies – where an account is given of the stewardship of these powers and people speak openly about how they perceive these powers are being exercised. "Accountability" in the Christian context includes a prior and proper accountability to God, who is the author and giver of every good gift; accountability to fellow Christians for mutual sharing, admonition, teaching and learning; and the common accountability of each member of the community to the good of the whole, which is shared particularly by those whose ministry entails responsibility for the *koinonia* as a whole.

The wise and constructive use of such occasions for communication may build up a sense of the common mind of the people of God (*sensus fidelium*). In Christian *koinonia* any exercise of authority is undergirded and judged by the presence of this *sensus fidelium* in all the members of the community. This spiritual perception, sense, discernment is the fruit of the indwelling of the Holy Spirit. Through it, baptized believers are enabled to recognize in the voice of the *episkopé* what is or is not an authentic echo of the voice of Christ, in the teaching of the community what is or is not in harmony with the truth of the gospel, in the decisions of those exercising *episkopé* what is or is not a real service of the common good of the church.

There is no absolute precision about which mode of government would protect the church completely from the occurrence of errors. In the present state of ecclesial disunity, strategies and occasions for mutual listening, encouragement and correction are needed. There is a necessary provisionality or tentativeness to decisions even of a legally competent body, affording time for due reflection. Especially in the context of the global village, consideration must be given to the integrity of the cultural traditions and norms of any given church and to its habits and processes for managing change.

Conclusion

The above reflections are offered to assist in the process of discerning and working on issues which concern our churches as they understand and practice oversight. It is hoped that they will be helpful for further theological reflections on *episkopé* in the local church, on continuity and the exercise of *episkopé* and episcopacy, on conciliarity and primacy.

These reflections have pointed to the fact that the way forward is often found within the way of renewal of church life and practice, that is, in identifying and addressing distortions in practice of what the churches teach about the ministry of oversight. We have devoted significant attention to the area of power because it is precisely in the use and abuse of power that the gifts and distortions of oversight find a fulcrum point.

TOWARDS COMMUNION IN *EPISKOPÉ* AND EPISCOPACY

Report of Group III

Introduction

In describing as "real but imperfect" the *koinonia* experienced by those churches which, in the words of the WCC Basis, "confess Jesus Christ as God and Saviour, to the glory of the one God, Father, Son and Holy Spirit", we point to the state of tension within which we live and work towards fuller visible unity. This group has reflected on how ecumenical dialogues and relationships, both in general and in particular about issues of *episkopé* and episcopacy, can be carried out fruitfully within this space of tension. These reflections have focused on (1) the characteristics of visible unity and how these are served by *episkopé;* (2) the gifts, strengths and limits to diversity within unity; (3) different levels and rates of progress in moves towards visible unity; (4) guidelines for coexistence and dialogue within this reality of tension, or "ecumenical space"; and (5) *episkopé* and episcopacy within ecumenical space.

Visible unity

As questions of *episkopé* and episcopacy are being raised within the context of the quest for full visible unity, it was considered helpful to relate our reflections to the parameters set forth in a particular portrait of visible unity. The statement of the WCC's seventh assembly (Canberra 1991) on "The Unity of the Church: Gift and Calling" seemed the most appropriate for our purposes.

1. Pointing the way

The Canberra statement describes the unity of the church as a *koinonia* given and expressed in
- the common confession of the apostolic faith;
- a common sacramental life entered by the one baptism and celebrated together in one eucharistic fellowship;

- a common life in which members and ministries are mutually recognized and reconciled;
- a common mission witnessing to the gospel of God's grace to all people and serving the whole of creation.

2. Unity, diversity and recognition

The goal of the search for full communion is realized when all the churches have been able to recognize in one another the one holy, catholic and apostolic church in its fullness, and to acknowledge that they are bound together at all levels in confessing the one faith, in worship and witness, deliberation and action.

Within this unity, diversity is essential; indeed, unity is served by diversity. The mutual exchange of gifts is one way in which diversity serves rather threatens unity. Yet it is also necessary to know what are the limits of diversity, so that we may have confidence in making a common confession of Jesus Christ and of the salvation and final destiny of humanity proclaimed in Holy Scripture.

3. Working with recognition and disagreement

The Canberra statement called the churches to a process which will include at least the following steps:
- to recognize each other's baptism on the basis of the *BEM* document;
- to move towards the recognition of the apostolic faith as expressed through the Nicene-Constantinopolitan Creed in the life and witness of one another;
- on the basis of convergence in faith in baptism, eucharist and ministry to consider, wherever appropriate, forms of eucharistic hospitality (with an acknowledgment that some who do not observe these rites share in the spiritual experience of life in Christ);
- to move towards the mutual recognition of ministries;
- to endeavour in word and deed to give common witness to the gospel as a whole;
- to recommit themselves to work for justice, peace and the integrity of creation, linking more closely the search for the sacramental communion of the church with the struggle for justice and peace;
- to help parishes and communities express locally in appropriate ways the degree of communion that already exists.

4. Issues of oversight

While not all churches can engage in this process at the same rate or in the same manner, it is important that their increasing ability to "walk together in mutual understanding, theological convergence, common suffering and common prayer, shared witness and service" be served by appropriate forms of *episkopé* at the various levels of the church's life – local, regional, worldwide. Nor should this concern for unity be merely geographical; it must also ensure the unity of the church today with the church of the apostles and throughout the ages.

Episkopé and episcopacy in their various forms are intended to express, witness to and serve the visible unity of the church.

Plurality in expressions of unity

This section explores the given reality of diversity, its legitimacy and the limits to it, then relates these points to the exercise of *episkopé* in the churches in their present divided state, even as they already manifest unity, albeit imperfectly.

In the diversity which characterizes the life of the divided churches it is not always easy to distinguish between differences arising on the one hand from the manifold gifts of the Spirit and the God-given diversity of human culture and experience, and those on the other hand whose source is "the spirit of this world" and which tend towards greater fragmentation and loss. Differences between denominations are of both kinds.

Among those who acknowledge Jesus Christ as God and Saviour there is a plurality in expressions of unity. This can be seen in the ways different churches and church families understand their own internal unity, consider moving towards unity with other churches and envisage the unity of the one church in time and space.

How do the churches move to a position where all can see in each other one and the same church and experience the visible unity of the church in its fullness? In this context, what is the relationship between unity and diversity?

Diversity is legitimate in the life of the church. It is not only a practical necessity but part of the God-given reality and richness of the unity to which all are called. As such, diversity has been experienced in the church from the beginning. "Unity in Christ does not exist despite and in opposition to diversity, but is given with and in diversity" (Roman Catholic-Lutheran Joint Commission, *Ways to Community*, 1981, para. 9).

But there are limits to diversity. According to the Canberra statement,

> diversity is illegitimate when... it makes impossible the common confession of Jesus Christ as God and Saviour, the same yesterday, today and for ever (Heb. 13:8); and salvation and the final destiny of humanity as proclaimed in holy scripture and preached by the apostolic community (para. 2.2).

Common liturgical celebration and shared life are signs of this common confession. The inability to worship together or to take common action is a sign of lack of agreement in faith and a counter-witness to the gospel. But appropriate diversity can be maintained and sustained through bonds of communion and mutual accountability. In the words of the Porvoo Common Statement:

> The maintenance of unity and the sustaining of diversity are served by bonds of communion. Communion with God and with fellow believers is manifested in one baptism in response to the apostolic preaching; in the common confession of the apostolic faith; in the united celebration of the eucharist which builds up the one body of Christ; and in a single ministry set apart by prayer and the laying on of hands. This unity is also manifested as a communion in love, implying that Christians are bound to one another in a committed relationship with mutual responsibilities, common spiritual goods and the obligation to share temporal resources (para. 24).

Unity by stages

As divided churches seek to be open to the gift of unity, they move at different speeds and by different means. This is inevitable, because of both differences in the issues that separate them and their complex histories. Thus the plurality which characterizes expressions of unity applies also to the process. It is important to develop an appropriate methodology for a unity which proceeds by stages, acknowledging that different sets of steps are needed because of the differing relationships between the divided churches. One possible way of characterizing these steps is as proceeding along a spectrum from conflict to competition, co-existence, comparison, co-operation, convergence/consensus, complementarity, commitment, conversion and finally communion.

Certain developments in the ecumenical movement, even very positive ones, have led to asymmetrical or anomalous relationships among the churches. This asymmetry has been created by several phenomena characteristic of the present era of church life:

- *Bilateral relationships.* The various paths and accents of the bilateral dialogues, the different doctrinal and historical issues dealt with and the reception of these dialogues have raised questions of consistency in theological articulation. Needed now is a forum in which underlying compatibility can be assessed and greater theological consistency attained.
- *Regional and national agreements.* Many regional and national agreements provide for the reconciliation of parts of world families of churches on the basis of regional ecclesial characteristics, without implying the reconciliation of whole world families of churches. This creates differences of pace and varieties of levels of reconciliation within the ecumenical movement.
- *Internal developments.* Developments within churches, such as the ordination of women and evolving styles of leadership, and responses to these developments are sources of both joy and pain. Developments for reasons of internal discipline and consistency have ecumenical resonance in the wider community because of our real but imperfect communion. All these factors vary the pace, context and climate in which the visible unity of the church can be achieved.
- *Political, economic and social imparities.* Inequalities between different parts of the world and within nations impose strains on all communities, including the churches. This can lead to fragmentation, to the marginalization of some groups within the ecumenical movement and to a multiplicity of theological discourses. All this can make mutual comprehension difficult.

Developing an appropriate milieu: "ecumenical space"

"Ecumenical space" is the milieu in which, even in a state of division, we bear witness to our common allegiance to Jesus Christ and cooperate to advance the visible unity of the church. In this space we affirm our common Christian identity. For this reason, we have the possibility of a new discourse: we talk to one another in a new way. In turn, we have a greater opportunity to discern together Christ's will for the church in ways that are not possible in isolation one from another. Space thus understood brings the churches into living encounter with one another. It is helpful to enumerate the presuppositions, characteristics, opportunities and obligations of being together in "ecumenical space".

Presuppositions of ecumenical space:
- recognition of common baptism in Christ;
- search for theological understanding on the basis of scripture, tradition and experience;

- commitment to search for unity, to seek to transcend former divisions;
- commitment to processes of dialogue, and thus to transformation and renewal in the light of the common quest;
- maintenance of fellowship in the situation of divergent affirmations, thus demonstrating commitment to the process.

Characteristics of ecumenical space:
- frank and serious discussion, including search and discovery, questioning and listening;
- mutual respect, so that no church is required to deny its identity or heritage;
- restraint from judgment, thus excluding a purely negative attitude on the part of one church towards another.

Opportunities afforded by ecumenical space:
- reconciliation of memories;
- conversion and renewal;
- common witness;
- guidance into the will of the Spirit;
- discernment of what will advance the visible unity of the church.

Obligations of being together in ecumenical space:
- compatibility of attitude and behaviour within and outside this ecumenical space;
- avoidance of actions inconsistent with brotherly/sisterly relationships;
- mutual support, forbearance and accountability.

Within such space, discernment takes place through testing on the basis of scripture, tradition and experience and according to confessional criteria. Individuals function as representatives of their communities committed to dialogue. Deliberation continues even when disagreements seem incapable of resolution. Ecumenical space continues to be a place of interrogation and encouragement, a place where the process of the reconciliation of history must occur.

The process of discernment within the space will raise questions about the relation between the global, regional and national processes of dialogue. It is clear that internal decisions cannot be reached in isolation from partners, and decisions in one region or nation will have an impact on others. For this reason, in any significant decision or agreement concerning church life, compatibility and consistency with partner churches should be tested before finalization. In sum, mutual accountability to partners must be a chief consideration in the stage-by-stage unfolding of a process that is under the Spirit and oriented to an ultimate future belonging to the Triune God.

Episkopé and episcopacy in ecumenical space

The need for an awareness and practice of "ecumenical space" is urgent now with regard to the topic of *episkopé*. The positive aspects of regional and bilateral agreements have allowed for a more focused ecumenical discussion, which has in turn advanced regional and bilateral forms of Christian unity. But, as we saw above, concerns have been raised that regional and bilateral agreements are also leading to an impairment of "real but imperfect communion" in other relationships, that is to an asymmetrical advance based on regional and bilateral models. Thus the requirement of an enhanced level of ecumenical oversight and mutual accountability is particularly urgent if the ecumenical movement is not to fragment along new fault lines.

Two questions inevitably arise in this situation:

1. Is there the possibility of ecumenical space allowing for a corporate exercise of *episkopé* and ecumenical accountability across the churches? Simply to speak of ecumenical space presupposes a certain capacity for transcendence on the part of individuals and churches, an openness to the concerns and insights of others and a sense of responsibility for others. Could this not be expressed in some structural form of *episkopé within* the ecumenical space?

2. Are there current institutional examples of ecumenical space? At present, councils of churches, multilateral dialogues, ecumenical institutes and associations, and joint meetings of those who exercise *episkopé* already provide ecumenical space. Is informal *episkopé* already being exercised in this space, which can now be defined more concretely? Within such space are both episcopal and non-episcopal churches able to question and listen to one another's experiences and reflections?

Some additional forms of ecumenical space must now be developed which participate in the *episkopé* of the churches if the variety of movements of the moment are to be coordinated in the direction of an encompassing visible unity of the one church.

Reflections

1. Are there affirmations about *episkopé*, viewed through the lens of ecumenical space, which emerge at the moment?

    a. a common emerging pattern of *episkopé* – perhaps even the emerging pattern of *episkopoi*,

    b. patterns of joint *episkopé*, which work best through the concept of unity by stages.

2. Viewed through the lens of ecumenical space, are there common dangers which regional and bilateral models are inadequate to confront?

    a. the influence of secular models of authority;

    b. the seductive forces of the media, which seek to impose on churches the need for representative persons to address issues of society authoritatively.

3. What is the protection against these potential dangers in the articulation of concrete models of ecumenical space?

    a. places in which models of *episkopé* can be evaluated in relation to the Word of God and the nature and purpose of the church;

    b. places in which it is possible to speak of exercising authority in an eschatological community;

    c. places which anchor *episkopé* in the whole church and in its mission beyond the horizon of regional or national bilateral arrangements.

REPORTS
FROM THE
CRÊT-BÉRARD CONSULTATION

5-11 SEPTEMBER 1997

COMMUNAL, COLLEGIAL, PERSONAL

Report of Group I

(**Note**: Certain paragraphs in this report have been taken from the report of Group II of the Strasbourg meeting.)

Introduction

It is always difficult for the church to speak about itself without slipping into the hubris of making the church a self-determining body. We realize with the Apostle that "now we see in a mirror, dimly" and "in part" (1 Cor. 13:12). But, though partial, what is seen in Christ is seen of God – and this is what gives us the courage to speak.

We affirm the need for oversight to preserve and maintain that unity in diversity and diversity in unity which are revealed in this "mirror" as God's desire for the reconciliation of all humankind. This is a missionary requirement. If the church wants to reflect God's design, it must find a way to be faithful to it. The ministry has developed as one of the principal means to serve this need. By *episkopé*, we understand a means of enabling such a ministry. But *episkopé* raises the question of authority.

There is only one correct and fruitful way to deal ecumenically with the thorny question of authority in the church, and that is to begin with a reflection on the mission and nature of the church of God on earth. This church is called to be a *koinonia*. Here and now this *koinonia* is realized in two radically inseparable realms. It is a *koinonia* with the triune God which is manifested, lived out and sustained through a *koinonia* that entails all categories of human diversity. It is at once a *koinonia* with God through a *koinonia* with other men and women, and a *koinonia* with other men and women through a *koinonia* with God. As long as these two essential constituent elements are not in osmosis, the church of God cannot be faithful to its vocation.

Ministry has to be understood at this junction of the two dynamisms constituting the *koinonia*, at the point where the divine dynamism of God's grace wants to embrace not only individuals but the human community as such. As expounded in the letter to the Ephesians, God's design is to sum up all things in Christ (Eph. 1:10), to make all Jews and Gentiles into one new humanity (2:15) by breaking down the dividing wall (2:14) and its barriers. As with everything in the church of God, ministry is essentially related to the nature of this divine purpose and necessarily related to the complexity of human diversity. For this divine plan concerns everyone. It must be "received" by everyone; it must affect the destiny of everyone.

But human diversity is in constant danger either of being transformed into deadly division or (in order to resist this eventuality) of being put under the pressure of tyranny, despotism and the absolutism which oppresses human freedom and destroys the native richness of fruitful differences. Consequently, it is not easy for the church on earth to be an authentic *koinonia*, in which unity does not threaten but promotes diversity, and diversity does not endanger but enhances unity. To grasp the meaning, the challenge and the necessity of the church's unity, the final verses of the gospel according to Matthew – "make disciples of all nations..., teaching them to obey everything that I have commanded you" (Matt. 28:19-20; cf. 24:14; 25:32; Acts 1:8) – are as necessary as the prayer of the Lord in the fourth gospel (John 17).

Being concretely realized in local churches, from really different races, conditions, cultures, traditions, histories, often separated by real ethnic or national interests, the church will be held together in a single *koinonia* by different means, among which ministries in communion have a specific role.

As was already expressed and widely agreed in *BEM*,

> the New Testament does not describe a single pattern of ministry which might serve as a blueprint or continuing norm for all future ministry in the church. In the New Testament there appears rather a variety of forms which existed at different places and times. As the Holy Spirit continued to lead the church in life, worship and mission, certain elements from this early variety were further developed and became settled into a more universal pattern of ministry (Ministry, para. 19).

Scripture and tradition together are the basis for this pattern. For example, St Ignatius of Antioch writes:

> All of you follow the bishop, as Jesus Christ followed the Father, and the presbytery as the Apostles; respect the deacons as the ordinance of God... Wherever the bishop shall appear, there let the people be; just as wherever Christ Jesus may be, there is the catholic church (*Smyrn.* 8, i-ii; cf. also *Trall.* 3,i; *Magn.* 6,i).

Although *BEM* spoke of this as a "threefold pattern", in the Western church at least that phrase is an over-simplification of the historical development. For example, there is uncertainty in some churches regarding a clear and final distinction between bishop and presbyter (for example, in Alexandria, as evident in the writings of St Jerome). However, a clear and normative pattern of sacramental *episkopé* exercised by the bishop emerged and prevailed in most areas of the church. According to this pattern, the bishop is the *ikon* (remembering that *ikon* and image are essentially synonymous) and sacramental presence of Christ. He presides over the one baptism and one eucharist of the church; he exercises a *charisma veritatis* and is called to be the guarantor of the truth; he passes on the ministries of the church as an expression of its *episkopé* and safeguards its apostolicity. The bishop represents the church and serves its unity, both synchronically and diachronically.

At the Reformation, the outcome of a long period of stresses and strains in church life, some Christian communities felt constrained to choose between loyalty to the episcopate of their time and fidelity to apostolic truth. Some churches installed new bishops outside the recognized line of episcopal succession, sometimes designating them by different terms. Others chose different structures of oversight, regarding this as a return to the primitive pattern of church life and ministry (conciliar leadership exercised by "*presbyteroi/episkopoi*").

A vital part of the modern ecumenical responsibility of the churches has been to seek a communion of ministries under the guidance and renewal of the Holy Spirit. Valued elements in this renewal have come from ancient tradition, from the insights of Reformation churches and from contemporary responses to new situations. The questions about ministry which face us here are not juridical questions about outward forms and order but questions about how the church of Jesus Christ can be obedient in ministry.

The renewed willingness today to engage this question for the sake of the mission, unity and wholeness of the church is characterized by:
- a letting go of the excluding judgments of the past;
- an openness to the guidance of the Holy Spirit for the future;
- willingness to share inheritances;
- a capacity to acknowledge deformations and bad examples from the past and in the present;
- new insights into the corporate reality of the life of the church, constituting a "common life/*koinonia*" through the redeeming blood of Christ (1 John 1);
- an understanding of the church as an eschatological sign of the kingdom of God.

As is clear from the report of the Strasbourg meeting which preceded the present consultation, it is helpful to understand the exercise of *episkopé* as personal, collegial and communal.

Diversity of gifts

In writing to the Corinthians (1 Cor. 12-14), Paul presents the church as a unity in diversity, a diversity which implies a hierarchy. This notion of hierarchy, which cannot be bypassed in a reflection on communal, collegial and personal dimensions at all levels in the life of the church, is not well received by most people in modern society. Indeed, the churches have too often exercised hierarchy in an equivocal, worldly way. In its use and understanding of power, the church too easily becomes *of* this world rather than *in* this world.

To understand the real Christian meaning of the term "hierarchy", we must remember that the tradition speaks of an order (*taxis*) within the Holy Trinity: we name the Father first, as the fountainhead of all divinity, then the Son as born from the Father, and then the Holy Spirit, as the one in whom God shines forth from all eternity. This "hierarchy" in no way means that any one of the three is less God than any of the others. They are the perfection of communion, the perfection of unity in diversity: absolute unity in no less absolute diversity – two absolutes, paradoxical as this may be. They are the model, the prototype of our unity in diversity or diversity in unity at all levels of the life of the church. In 1 Corinthians 12 we find an hierarchical order in which all members of the body are nevertheless firmly invited to live in mutual service and love.

Understood in this way, hierarchy is not a matter of domination and submission. It is in this light that the church should understand the nature of its own hierarchy, even if Christians more often than not tend to forget this essential element of their existence as a community and their witness to the non-Christian world. According to this view, the church is a communion of co-responsible persons. It is evident that no function, no gift, no charisma, is exercised outside or *above* this communion. All are related in one Spirit, and through the Body.

In the New Testament, *exousia* and *dynamis* are used interchangeably in the context of authority. It is in the exercise of creative and salvific power that the authority of God is manifested. Christians live under the authority of God because the resources of God's power are open to them. The eleven wait to be armed with "power from on high", the gift of the Holy Spirit (Luke 24:49; cf. Acts 1:8), through which they will receive authority together with the power to witness with boldness and conviction. There is no true authority in the church which is not energized by the power for its right exercise. For instance, the apostle Paul, though acutely feeling his own weakness, nevertheless speaks the word of truth powerfully and wants to use his authority constructively to build up his quarrelling congregation (2 Cor. 13).

This is power of a very particular kind. Like the power of the Lord himself, it is vulnerable power, which refuses the sword and legions of angels (Matt. 26:52), which is a power to lay down one's life (John 10:18) and which persists until the great work of redemption is finished (John 19:30). It is a power which reverses the order of the world, putting down the mighty and raising up the humble (Luke 1:52). It is a power by which Jesus Christ, *because* he humbled himself and was obedient to death, received the supreme authority of Lord, being exalted and given the name above every name (Phil. 2:5-11). The power and authority of the transcendent God, and therefore the work of every form of power and authority in the church, take the way of the cross and live under its sign.

The basis for our concept and exercise of *episkopé* should be Christ's words:

> The kings of the Gentiles lord it over them; and those in authority over them are called benefactors. But not so with you; rather the greatest among you must become like the youngest, and the leader like one who serves. For who is greater, the one who is at the table or the one who serves? Is it not the one at the table? But I am among you as one who serves (Luke 22:25-27; see also Matt. 20:25-28; Mark 9:35; 10:42-45).

Yet at the Last Supper itself, according to Luke's account, a dispute arose over which of them should be considered greatest (Luke 22:24). Jesus' statement, "I am among you as one who serves" (Luke 22:27), and his example of washing his disciples' feet (John 13:2-17) permanently challenge the church in every age to interrogate its own uses of power and exercise of authority, lest the love of money and strategies of domination intrude upon its performance of the tasks of leadership (1 Pet. 5:1-4).

In this perspective, our conception of the church must be one which starts from something evident from the beginning. It must consist in struggling to resist all forms of worldly domination, so that the church may tend to be that "prophetic sign" which may heal the world instead of giving way to it.

Together with the Acts of the Apostles (2:42-47; 4:32-35), the instructions of Jesus concerning relations among those who wish to be disciples represent the indisputable foundation of the community which claims to be the Body of Christ under the authority of Christ, its Head. It is a life in communion in which there is no room for the domination-submission relation. No one is *above* this communion but all, whatever their functions, are *within* it.

Communal - collegial - personal

Among the fundamental New Testament texts essential for our reflection on what the church is, is 1 Peter 2:5, in which we are called as "living stones" to be "built into a spiritual house". In such a perspective, personal, communal and collegial outworkings of oversight are very closely interrelated.

1. Communal

Because the church is the Body of Christ, the service of God's design has a communal character. All baptized members must take seriously their potential to exercise the gifts they receive from the Holy Spirit – never for their own sake alone, but for the life and mission of the whole community.

Among these gifts are the gifts of diverse ministries in each sphere of the church's life. Already in the New Testament there is evidence that this service (*diakonia*) of the community is diverse (including apostles, prophets, teachers, etc.; cf. 1 Cor. 12). But it is clear that, for the sake of God's design, all these services are to be exercised in communion. Moreover, they must reflect the concern of the whole community under the guidance of the Holy Spirit. For example, the outcome of the meeting (Acts 15) of the apostles and elders (*presbyteroi*), provoked by the problems of the local communities in their Gentile and Palestinian contexts, is through a coming together of persons chosen and appointed by the churches on account of their stature and qualities of leadership (*hegoumenoi*) and "with the consent of the whole church" (Acts 15:22). In this *synodos* we discern a foreshadowing of synodality (conciliarity). In the church of God, ministry is communal.

2. Collegial

Tradition would inscribe what it called episcopacy as a specific ministry within this communal service in the church. Although it can be and has been betrayed at times, this ministry should still be recognized as a gift. Hence the necessary collegial dimension of leadership among those who have been chosen by their church to exercise this charge of oversight. We remember that in the New Testament it is to the groups of the apostles *as a whole* that Christ gave the commission to preach the gospel and lead the church. Other disciples would share in this mission (Matt. 28:1-10, 16-20; John 20). What Paul says of each member of the Body of Christ – that they should care for one another (1 Cor. 12:25) – is true also of ministry. This is shown, for example, in the ministry of Mary Magdalene to the disciples (John 20).

None can take account only of the interests of their own community. The practical implications of working as fellow-servants have to do with the mutual dealings of all the communities in the same gospel, in ways comparable with that shown by the collection for the saints in Jerusalem (2 Cor. 9; Gal. 2:10).

3. Personal

Like the collegial, the personal aspect is included in the communal. Regarding this dimension of *episkopé, BEM* stated that the exercise of ordained ministry should be *personal* because the presence of Christ among his people can most effectively be pointed to by the person ordained to proclaim the gospel and to call the community to serve the Lord in unity of life and witness (Ministry, para. 26).

The presence of Christ among his people is pointed to by the ministry of a person ordained to be the sacrament of the Lord's episcopacy. The term "pointed to" alludes to the words of John the Baptist in the fourth gospel (John 1:19-30). Personal eclipse and personal service are to be held together, since the supreme *episkopos* is Christ. The calling of an ordained minister is to service and responsibility within the body of Christ. We describe this as a *personal* ministry, not an *individual* ministry. "Person" cannot be understood outside of the links with the community.

Bishops or their equivalent are said to be *ikons* or images of Christ, acting *in persona Christi*. As images of the glorified Lord, they are images of Christ the servant, who set his disciples an example by washing their feet (John 13:14-15). As all human beings, they are dependent upon the grace of God, through the power of the Holy Spirit bestowed in Christ Jesus, hence the source of their own authority. They receive the anointing of the same Spirit, who animates the life of all believers, and are inseparably bound to them. Thus they should not be exalted above the community, and should point to the unique mediatorial work of Christ, not to themselves.

Within and together with the community, the *episkopos* or equivalent is involved in discerning vocations and in ordaining other ministers to share in Christ's mission through the ministry of Word and Sacrament. These tasks, together with that of discipline, are a central way in which they exercise, in communion, care for the unity, faithfulness in truth and nurture of the people of God. In churches which do not have named bishops, these tasks are likewise carried out by persons bearing responsibility for *episkopé*. In all cases the intention is reverently to esteem and to continue the office given by Christ to the church, through prayer for the sending of the Holy Spirit and the laying on of hands. In all cases the congregations are explicitly involved in and invited to consent to the act, and to join in prayer for the candidates.

In Christian *koinonia* any exercise of authority is undergirded and judged by the presence of the *sensus fidelium* in all the members of the community. This spiritual perception, sense, discernment is the fruit of the indwelling of the Holy Spirit. Through it, baptized believers are enabled to recognize in the voice of the *episkopos* what is or is not an authentic echo of the voice of Christ, in the teaching of the community what is or is not in harmony with the truth of the gospel, in the decisions of those exercising *episkopé* what is or is not a real service of the common good of the church.

All that has been said about life in communion applies to local Christian communities, provincial, regional and national groups of churches and their worldwide manifestation.

EPISKOPÉ, EPISCOPACY AND APOSTOLIC CONTINUITY

Report of Group II

What initiates and sustains the life of the people of God throughout the ages is God's faithfulness, God's creative Word, God's effective promise (Gen. 1:1-28; 12:1-3; Matt. 16:28; 28:20). The faithful sustaining of the people of God is brought about by outward means of grace received through inward activity of the Holy Spirit. In this way the church is kept within apostolic continuity. All churches agree that being apostolic in this sense belongs to the definition of the church. All regard themselves as being apostolic church.

The gifts of grace by which God sustains the church are an expression of God's initiative: gospel (*kerygma*), sacraments, the ordained ministry which serves as an instrument of conferring them. The response from the human side is a life in faith, love and witness. God uses this response as a vehicle for handing down the means of apostolicity; it serves the apostolic continuity of the church. Yet while evoked by the Holy Spirit, the human response is susceptible to all the characteristics of the human condition.

Although all churches would agree with this basic understanding of apostolicity, the ways in which they identify the means of maintaining apostolic continuity differ. In brief, there are clear differences among the churches in how they understand (1) what are the means of maintaining apostolic continuity, (2) how they are interrelated, (3) the degree to which they participate in the continuity promised to the church, (4) how apostolic continuity depends on them. An overarching reason for these differences lies in the ways in which they describe the relationship between God's initiative and the response to it from the human side in the history of the church.

The church *in via* (that is between the incarnation and the *parousia* of Jesus Christ) interprets and embodies the gospel in history, which is the drama of the human condition in space and time. Being *in via* means that the church participates in the ambiguity of human perception, experience and activity. For some churches, the understanding of this ambiguity also entails sin.

During history, in different circumstances and cultural contexts, the church has developed several instruments for the handing on of apostolic truth through time, among them scriptural canon, dogma, liturgical order and institutional structures above the level of the local communities. While all these relate not only to the basic means of apostolicity but also to each other, we shall concentrate here on institutional structures above the level of the local community, that is, *episkopé*.

Over the course of the first centuries of the Christian church, communion between local congregations (which had existed in such informal yet significant links as visits, letters and collections) became more and more institutionalized. Two main structures that emerged were episcopacy and synods on different levels. Their purpose was to hold the local congregations in communion, to defend and hand down apostolic truth, to provide mutual support, to witness together to the gospel. All these functions are usually summed up in the term *episkopé*.

The specific development of structures of *episkopé* – both synods and episcopacy – varied in different regions of the church. The crystallization of most of the episcopal functions in the hands of one individual (*episkopos*) was much later in some places than in others, for example, Ireland, Scotland and regions affected by the missionary work of the Celtic church. In every case, however, what is understood or evident is that *episkopé* and episcopacy are in the service of maintaining continuity in apostolic truth.

This interrelatedness of episcopacy and apostolic truth came to be problematic at particular times for certain areas of the church. Thus, for example, the Reformers saw themselves as having to choose between fidelity to the *episkopoi* of the time and fidelity to apostolic truth. Although this alternative was occasionally mitigated when a bishop accepted the Reformation, in most cases the churches of the Reformation either installed new bishops or, having experienced the break between apostolic truth and *episkopoi* as systemic, adopted another structure of *episkopé*. For the Reformers, this choice was the way of continuity in apostolic truth, whereas those who remained with the existing *episkopoi* considered their choice as maintaining such continuity.

Aspects of this experience of having to choose between different elements and understandings of apostolic continuity can be seen whenever the church has suffered temporary or lasting division: in disputes over the baptism of heretics, in councils of the fourth and fifth centuries, in the iconoclastic crisis, in conflicts about papal primacy. Thus, the conflict over episcopacy and episcopal succession can be seen as a specific expression of a more general reality, which has to do with the ambiguity inherent in the church's history in so far as it participates in the general condition of humankind.

The ecumenical heritage of these differing experiences and theological interpretations is that churches for whom episcopacy and episcopal succession are essential to apostolic continuity live today alongside other churches who regard any specific shape of *episkopé* as variable and relative to continuity in apostolic truth. By contradicting each other at this point, both sides diminish or even deny each other's claims to be church in apostolic continuity.

While it has not yet been possible to overcome this divergence, there has been a growing recognition of openings which might lead to convergence:

- the recognition of the interdependence of each other's histories, polities, theologies;
- new insights achieved through dialogue and the experience of living together;
- recognition of shortcomings within one's own ecclesial structure and practice, appreciation of the strengths evident in that of the others;
- the admission by each of sin in nurturing and sustaining attitudes and practices which deny the apostolic integrity of the others;
- the awareness that on all sides institutional continuity is recognized as being at the service of, and in that sense subordinate to, continuity in apostolic truth.

This has led certain churches to a new appreciation of oversight in personal forms, whereas other churches have come to a new appreciation of the integration of the episcopal office into the context of the apostolicity of the whole church.

Apostolicity, Continuity and Sign

Report of Group III

Ecumenical background

1. Baptism, Eucharist and Ministry (BEM)

To assist the churches towards the goal of visible church unity, the Faith and Order Commission has for more than fifty years directed its attention to the topics of baptism, eucharist and ministry. A decisive stage in this process of study, consultation and collaboration between Faith and Order and the churches was the publication in 1982 of *Baptism, Eucharist and Ministry*.

Of immediate importance in the context of the present study on *episkopé* and episcopacy is an exploration of how *BEM* employed the terminology of "sign" in regard to the topic of ministry. In the first two sub-sections of the Ministry portion of *BEM* ("The Calling of the Whole People of God" and "The Church and the Ordained Ministry), the word or concept "sign" is not mentioned. But in the third sub-section ("The Forms of the Ordained Ministry"), the text says about the ministry of unity (*episkopé*): "Every church needs this ministry in some form in order to be the church of God, the one body of Christ, a sign of the unity of all in the kingdom" (para. 23). And in the fourth section ("Succession in the Apostolic Tradition"), it is said that "this succession was understood as serving, symbolizing and guarding the continuity of the apostolic faith and communion" (para. 36). The text goes on to say that

> These considerations... enable the churches which have not retained the episcopate to appreciate the episcopal succession as a sign, though not guarantee, of the continuity and unity of the church. Today churches... are expressing willingness to accept episcopal succession as a sign of the apostolicity of the life of the whole church (para. 38).

In the fifth section ("Ordination"), it is stated that "the laying on of hands is the sign of the gift of the Spirit, rendering visible the fact that the ministry was instituted in the revelation accomplished in Christ..." (para. 39). Furthermore, "the act of ordination by the laying on of hands of those appointed to do so is at one and the same time invocation of the Holy Spirit (*epiklesis*); sacramental sign; acknowledgment of gifts and commitment" (para. 41). Ordination is a sign of God's initiative (paras 42 and 43). Thus ordination is a sign performed in faith.

Finally, in the sixth section ("Towards the Mutual Recognition of Ordained Ministries"), the text states that churches without the episcopal succession "may need to recover the sign of episcopal succession" (para. 53b).

While it is not the intention here to present a study of *BEM*'s use of the word "sign", its appearance in the other two parts of *BEM* may be mentioned briefly. Baptism is described as a sign of new life, of the kingdom of God, of the gift of the Spirit. Mutual recognition of baptism is an important sign of baptismal unity. Various actions connected with baptism, anointing and laying on of hands, are signs. Likewise the eucharist is a sacramental meal which by visible signs communicates God's love in Christ. It is the living and effective sign of Christ's sacrifice. The bread and wine become the sacramental signs of Christ's body and blood.

2. Responses to BEM

Only a relatively small number of the responses of the churches to *BEM* mention the concepts of "sign" or "guarantee" at all. Some churches, among them the Seventh-day Adventists, ask for further clarification. Those which do take up these concepts express a range of views. For example, several churches were pleased to acknowledge the episcopal succession as a "sign of unity and continuity". Yet among these a significant portion – Berlin-Brandenburg, Uniting Church in Australia, Methodist Church (UK), Evangelical Church of the Rhineland – noted that they could not apply the notion of "guarantee" in this context. Others, primarily the Roman Catholic Church and some Orthodox (e.g., Inter-Orthodox Symposium, Russian Orthodox Church), felt that "sign" by itself is insufficient to express the reality without saying also that episcopal succession guarantees unity and continuity. There were also churches (e.g., Waldensian and Methodist churches in Italy, Evangelical Church of the Rhineland) which indicated that no minister or ministry "could express or safeguard the unity of the body", or that ordination is "not a sacramental sign" but an "act of dedication to the service of the Word of God". Interestingly, some churches (Independent Evangelical Lutheran Church (FRG), Russian Orthodox Church) found it questionable or impossible to single out the apostolicity of ministry from that of the entirety of the church's life.

Issues of apostolic continuity

1. The apostolicity of the church

Apostolicity entails the message of God's good news. It belongs to the life of the people of God – to the church. Jesus Christ was sent by the Father to make known and to bring to completion the divine purpose of salvation. The church can be described as apostolic in two senses: (a) it is historically founded by and still rests on the apostles Jesus sent and on their witness to him; and (b) it is "apostled", sent out, in every generation. The divine mission continues in and through the church from the apostles onwards. Apostolicity is founded on Christ's fidelity to his promise to be always with his people, through the action of the Holy Spirit, and on the response of the people of God living in fidelity to the faith, life and mission of the apostles. The church is given the gift of God's fidelity in order that it will be itself faithful. This fidelity of God which inspires the faithful response of the people of God constitutes the apostolic succession of the church.

Responsibility for maintaining the apostolicity of the church – its proclamation of the gospel, its life and mission – is shared by all the people of God in every time and in every place. In every generation the church is historically particular and has to meet the changes and needs of the world and to preserve its life in the contingencies of the world. The church is sustained in its perseverance in truth by Christ's promise – even though its unity, fidelity and peace are constantly vulnerable. The ultimate safeguard of the church's apostolicity from generation to generation is the assurance of the action of the Holy Spirit.

The apostolicity of the church cannot be separated from its mission of offering itself for the life of the world. The apostolicity of the church entails embracing the mission of God's suffering and vulnerable love. The vocation of the church is to be a credible and a "prophetic sign" of the kingdom of God.

2. The gifts of apostolicity

Like any visible community the church needs recognizable signs or characteristics of its identity, as well as instruments to sustain and maintain its identity and unity. These distinctive signs and instruments ensure that continuity is recognized from place to place and from generation to generation. Among the characteristics and instruments of its unity and continuity in the apostolic mission and life are the continuous transmission of the holy scriptures, the celebration of the sacraments, the faith confessed in the creeds and borne witness to in confessional statements, the care for the community and the world, and the service of ministry.

Within the total life of the church, the gifts of apostolic continuity form parts of a single system of identity, a single system of communication. The various gifts or elements of apostolicity nurture the local church. They also link local churches to one another, as well as linking the local churches to the apostles. The gifts of the holy scriptures, sacraments, creeds, pastoral care and ministry link past, present and future generations. The churches are called to remain faithful from generation to generation. Apostolicity requires openness to the Holy Spirit, correction under the Spirit's guidance and constant re-interpretation to meet the needs of new situations. It needs constant turning to Christ and repentance.

3. Apostolicity and ministry

Every member of the church has a responsibility for maintaining the apostolicity of the church. Various gifts are given to share in and build up the life and apostolic mission of the church. Every member is dependent on the Holy Spirit for the gifts and for their faithful, life-long exercise in the service of the church and of the world.

In, with and among the life of the people of God, the ordained ministry is called out by God, through the church, for a service of strengthening and building up the apostolic life of the church. To ordained ministry belongs oversight of the community in the service of apostolicity. The ordained ministry is relational, entailing a relationship both to Christ (*in persona Christi*) and to the community (*in persona ecclesiae*); thus, the ordained person is called to represent both Christ and the community.

4. Ordination as a sign of apostolicity

In ordination the people of God affirm their belief that the persons to be ordained are indeed called by God and know themselves to be called by God. In ordination God's promise of the Holy Spirit is claimed for the exercise of the particular ministry and office in the church. When the word "sign" is used of the act of ordination, it has a multi-faceted meaning. The laying on of hands, together with the prayer of the community calling upon the action of the Holy Spirit, is a sign for the church that a special gift is being bestowed by God on the one ordained for a particular service in the church, that the community relies on God's promise of the Holy Spirit to be with his people, that the one ordained trusts in the gift of the Spirit for the carrying out of a particular ministry, and that the community recognizes the call and intends to cooperate with and support the one being ordained to that particular ministry and office. Ordination is further a sign that the whole community – ordained and lay together – relying on the gift of the Holy Spirit, intends to be faithful to the apostolic faith, life and mission of the church.

The use of the word "sign" in this way refers not to an "empty sign", a "mere sign". It refers to the unending promise of the gift of the Holy Spirit, God's promise to be always with the church and the promise to be with the person being ordained. The sign of ordination assures those ordained that they are being given the charge of ministry. While it cannot ensure in any mechanical or quasi-magical way the fidelity of the individual so ordained, it nevertheless strengthens that person for service through the gift of the Holy Spirit. The ambiguity and frailty of the human condition in the response to that gift always remain.

Nothing the people of God do can take away the divine promise of presence. In this sense, the "sign" of ordination can be said to be an "effective" sign, for it points to a reality which is a divine, assured reality. The sign also points to the church's intention to be faithful to the apostolic teaching and mission. When the word "guarantee" is used of the sign of ordination, it emphasizes both the continuing faithfulness of the Lord of the church to be with the church to the end of time and the intention of the church to be faithful. It is an assurance of the permanent and abiding presence of God's gift for sustaining the one ordained in office.

5. A ministry of oversight in the service of apostolicity

Among the gifts of ministry is a particular function of oversight (*episkopé*), recognized and distributed differently in different churches. The service of the apostolicity of the church entails a ministry of oversight in mission, in ministry of Word and Sacrament, in worship and praise, in guardianship of the faith, in declaring forgiveness of sins, in discipline and in commissioning for ministry. The ministry of oversight itself is entrusted to the whole church. Those to whom the function of oversight is entrusted by God and the community are called to exercise it in, with and among the whole community, and in a special way in solidarity with all who are entrusted with oversight. Thus the ministry of oversight is exercised in a communal, personal and collegial way.

Until the Reformation the ministry of oversight in both East and West was pre-eminently exercised by the bishops of local churches, who were concerned also with the care and oversight of all the churches, shared through a collegial relationship of bishops. That relationship also connected the church in one generation to another. This was demonstrated in the act of ordination by three or more bishops who had themselves been ordained by bishops in continuity of episcopal ordinations. This represents the diachronic and synchronic unity, continuity and solidarity of the church.

At the Reformation, different patterns of the ministry of oversight emerged. Continuity was more often signified in the Reformation churches through presbyteral ordinations. Some believed that fidelity to the apostolic truth, safeguarding and maintaining the apostolicity of the church, required a break with the succession of ministry. The Reformers sought to preserve the apostolicity of the church in varying ways. Some maintained the apostolic ministry of episcopal oversight, but abandoned or were unable to retain the form of a sign of episcopal order and succession, maintaining continuity rather through presbyteral succession. Others subsequently regained an episcopal order, though with a break in the form and sign of a continuous succession.

Some non-episcopal churches claim a historic succession in ministry. Every Presbyterian minister, for example, receives the apostolic commission through ordination by presbytery. Likewise, Methodists are accepted by the conference and ordained by the president or presiding bishop and ministers acting under the authority of the conference. These churches hold that there is in them an historical succession through a corporate body.

6. Historic episcopal succession as a sign of apostolicity

Historic episcopal succession – ordination in intended continuity with the apostles – consisted not in a chain of those ordaining apart from the life of the whole church, but in the succession in the ministry of oversight of a church which itself stands in the continuity of apostolic faith and is overseen by the bishop, whose vocation is to maintain the apostolicity of the church. Faithfulness to the apostolic calling is carried by more than one means of continuity. Apostolic succession is not the private, personal possession of a bishop, enjoyed in isolation from the local church:

> Apostolicity inheres not in the person of the bishop alone, but in the local church as a whole; and so apostolic succession means not simply the unbroken succession of *persons*, but the unbroken continuity of *communities*. There is no true succession of persons that is not mediated through the community.[1]

Just as the sign of ordination does not ensure the fidelity of the one being ordained, so also the sign of historic episcopal succession does not and cannot ensure the fidelity of a church to every aspect of the faith, life and mission of the apostles. Nevertheless, historic episcopal succession remains an effective sign of the presence of the Holy Spirit with the church through the ages, a permanent challenge to fidelity and unity, a summons to witness to and a commission to realize more fully the permanent characteristics of the church of the apostles, an assurance to the faithful that the church intends to preach the faith and celebrate the sacraments in continuity and in communion with the church of all places and all times.

A challenge to the churches

The challenge made in *BEM* needs reiterating with greater urgency:

> a. Churches which have preserved the episcopal succession are asked to recognize both the apostolic content of the ordained ministry which exists in churches which have not maintained such succession and also the existence in these churches of a ministry of *episkopé* in various forms.
>
> b. Churches without the episcopal succession, and living in faithful continuity with the apostolic faith and mission, have a ministry of word and sacrament, as is evident from the belief, practice and life of those churches. These churches are asked to realize that continuity with the church of the apostles finds profound expression in the successive laying on of hands by bishops and that though they may not lack the continuity of the apostolic tradition, this sign will strengthen and deepen that continuity. They may need to recover the sign of episcopal succession (Ministry, para. 53).

A single ministry of oversight within the life of the visibly united church would enable and help the church to live together a life of faith and sacraments, to take counsel together, to take common decisions, to teach together with conviction and to engage together in service and in mission so that the world may believe.

Churches which understand themselves to have retained the historic episcopate have explained the retention of episcopacy and commended it to those churches which do not have bishops in the historic episcopal succession. Those churches which do not have bishops have in their turn explained why they have not retained this ministry. As the report of Group I of the Strasbourg meeting shows, episcopal churches have begun to treat more critically some of the weaknesses in their theologies and practices of the ministry of oversight – some of which undermined a credible apologetic for episcopacy and succession – and should continue to do so. The churches which have not retained the office of bishops and the sign of historic succession have been challenged to consider the value of episcopacy and should continue to do so.

NOTE

[1] Kallistos Ware, in *Returning Pilgrims: Insights from British and Irish Participants in the Fifth World Conference on Faith and Order*, London, CCBI, 1994, pp.30f.

PAPERS
FROM THE
STRASBOURG CONSULTATION

About the authors

Jean-Marie R. Tillard, O.P. is Professor of Dogmatic Theology at the Dominican Faculty, Ottawa, Canada, and at the University of Fribourg, Switzerland. He is a vice-moderator of the Faith and Order Commission and a member of the Joint International Commission for the Theological Dialogue between the Roman Catholic Church and the Orthodox Church, of the Anglican-Roman Catholic International Commission, of the International Commission for Dialogue between the Catholic Church and the Disciples of Christ.

John H. Erickson is professor of canon law and church history and associate dean for academic affairs at St Vladimir's Orthodox Theological Seminary, Crestwood, New York. He is a member of the North American Orthodox-Roman Catholic Theological Consultation and the Faith and Order Commission of the National Council of Churches of Christ in the USA.

Gao Ying is an ordained minister in the China Christian Council, and teaches ecumenics at Nanjing Theological Seminary. She is on the executive committee of the Beijing Council of Churches.

Stephen Sykes is bishop of Ely, and principal-designate of St John's College, Durham. He chairs the Church of England's Doctrine Commission and the House of Bishops Theological Group, and was a member of the Porvoo Conversation.

Hugh Cross is retired ecumenical moderator of the Milton Keynes Christian Council, Milton Keynes, England.

Penny Jamieson is the Anglican bishop of Dunedin, Aotearoa New Zealand. She was a member of the Eames Commission on Women and the Episcopate. Another version of this paper appears in *Episcopacy: Views from the Antipodes*, edited by Alan Cadwallader and David Richardson, and published by the Joint Board of Christian Education, Collingwood, Australia.

Martin H. Cressey, retired principal of Westminster College, Cambridge, is a member of the Faith and Order Standing Commission and was moderator of the Fifth and Sixth International Consultations of United and Uniting Churches.

1. EPISCOPACY:
A GIFT OF THE SPIRIT

J.M.R. Tillard, O.P.

I

In the Catholic Church, as in the Orthodox churches and certain circles of the churches of the Reformation, the question of *institution* is bound up with the equally complex question of the nature of the episcopacy. This is linked in turn with the ecumenical discussions of apostolic succession. What is known as the ecclesial institution is the stable structure, remaining the same through the centuries, in which and thanks to which the *communion* of all believers among themselves and with the Father, in Christ, is ensured. Through it, the divine plan of salvation is embodied not in a vague number of isolated individuals brought together by grace but in a community organized in accordance with the specific goal expressed in the letter to the Ephesians as making up the Body of which Christ is the Head (Eph. 1:22-23), gathering torn humanity together again in the *eirene* of God (2:13-17), building together a habitation for God through the Spirit (2:22). The Reformation as such did not want to abolish but to reform the institution.

To be sure – as Augustine in the West never ceases to repeat – the Body of Christ and the Temple of God are realities over which the Spirit alone has dominion. The limits of the institution do not necessarily coincide with the extension of the Body of the Lord or the dimensions of the Temple. From Augustine's many statements on the *corpus permixtum,* let us cite these lines:

> Do not be surprised by the multitude of bad Christians who fill the church, who participate at the altar... In the church of this time they may be with us, but in that assembly of the saints which will come after the resurrection they will not be found. The church of this time is similar indeed to a threshing floor where grain and chaff are mixed,

where the wicked mingle with the good; after the judgment, it will include all the good, with none of the wicked. This threshing floor holds the harvest sown by the Apostles..., which the persecution of its enemies has beaten only a little, but... which has not yet been sifted by the winnowing from on high. He will come, however, the one of whom we have proclaimed in the Creed, "He will come again to judge the living and the dead". And as the gospel says, *His winnowing fork is in his hand, and he will clear his threshing floor and gather his wheat into the granary, but the chaff he will burn with unquenchable fire* (Matt. 3:12).[1]

On the other hand, Augustine explains that the Lord and his Spirit know those who, outside the institution, are already in salvation.[2] Nevertheless, it falls to the institution to offer, guarantee, manifest and maintain for all the set of instruments of salvation in which the power of the Spirit is exerted. These are the proclaiming and teaching of the Word, the celebration of the sacraments, above all the eucharist, and the "cure of souls", as a beautiful Reformed expression has it. The institution has the mission of making it possible for every person who desires to find the means of sanctification in the *koinonia*. The Code of Canon Law of January 1983 specifies at some length the rights of the faithful (canons 211-231) and, correlatively, the strict duty of the institution to answer to those rights. This signifies an official acknowledgment of the nature of the institution.

Indeed, it is not simply a matter of each believer finding, if God wills, available and generous people who agree benevolently to aid him or her in living his or her Christian vocation. The institution is a socially constituted reality, recognized as the setting of the life in communion to which it gives visibility. As such, it confers on the availability and generosity of specifically designated representatives a consistency which is protected from and transcends all the hazards of individual good will. It guarantees a stability in the service of the means of salvation. For this service as embodied in the institution, specific activities are established in a fixed way and are as it were mobilized in accordance with the *koinonia* to be realized. This implies persons officially consecrated for this service, formally recognized as such, organized in accordance with it, granted the authority that such service demands. This authority possesses power enough to be effective, which is made concrete either by legislation adapted to the common good and the good of individuals or by specific means of action marked out by that legislation.

Let us be clear on this point. Bringing this ensemble into play requires an administrative apparatus and suggests the creation of certain "institutions" (the catechumenate, theological schools, seminaries and so on). But that is not essential to the ecclesial *institution* as we are presenting it here. The *institution* is not to be confused with either the administration it necessitates or with the "institutions" it gives rise to. It is the setting of the life in *communion*, its framework, its support, and that which ensures its growth in faith and sacramental life. We like to define it as the expression of *koinonia* at once in its continuity, its structure and its dependence on faith and sacrament with regard to God.

Thus defined, the institution of the church rests on the episcopacy. Not without reason, the theology of the traditions known as "Catholic" connect this certainty with the rich affirmation of the letter to the Ephesians:

The gifts he gave were that some would be apostles, some prophets, some evangelists, some pastors and teachers, to equip the saints for the work of ministry, for building up the body of Christ, until all of us come to the unity of the faith and of the knowledge of the Son of God, to maturity, to the measure of the full stature of Christ. We must no longer be children, tossed to and fro and blown about by every wind of doctrine, by people's trickery, by their craftiness in deceitful scheming. But speaking the truth in love, we must grow up in every way into him who is the head, into Christ, from whom the whole body, joined and knit together by every ligament with which it is equipped, as each part is working properly, promotes the body's growth in building itself up in love (4:11-16).[3]

God gave (*edōken*) Christ to the church as its Head (Eph. 1:22-33); Christ in his turn "gave" (*edōken*) to the church the ministers necessary for its upbuilding into the Body of Christ (4:11-12).

Just as Christ did not resurrect himself, so the church does not provide itself with the needed men on its own initiative. It is endowed, it depends on the Lord and on this gracious and thus sovereign, sovereign and thus gracious, gift... The apostles are clearly separated and distinguished from prophets and followers... In conformity with a unanimous teaching, the choice of the apostles constitutes a founding initiative which depends on the Lord alone. Later functions derive from the first.[4]

The church is ceaselessly "sent back to the gospel", thanks to the ministers given by Christ.[5]

The nucleus of what we call the institution is there. Now, what is the specific function of these *human* "gifts" who are ministers? It is the perfecting, the equipping (*katartismos*), of the faithful as authentic adults in the faith, and their gathering into the one Body of Christ (4:12-13), knit together by knowledge of the Son of God, in love (4:15). The goal seems indeed to be the full stature of the church.[6] For it is in this way that the church, as Body of Christ, receives harmonious growth from its Head, its various parts finding themselves articulated, adjusted and coordinated according to their nature. These *human* "gifts" structure it visibly.

It is this mission of the original ministry which is pursued in the episcopacy and the other ministerial functions deriving from or attached to it. Here too it is a matter of the gracious *gift* that God gives to his church for its life and growth into the Body of Christ – but always starting from Christ the Head and in reference to the full eschatological realization of the Father's plan. Already at the time of the pastoral epistles it was recognized that those whom the apostle chose to be his companions in ministry and those who would continue the apostolic mission – in so far as it is transmissible, for there is an *ephapax* of the witness of those who saw the Risen One and "accompanied us" (Acts 1:21) – received the specific gift of the Spirit precisely for this service by the laying on of hands (1 Tim. 4:14; 2 Tim. 1:6). The epistles to Timothy and Titus show that what was involved was a charisma of government – thus already an institution – with the right and power to teach and prescribe (1 Tim. 4:11-12) in order to keep the community on the right path. Indeed, with the difficulties that were beginning to arise, something like a ministerial company was needed, allowing for the confirmation of the faithful in faith and charity but also watching over all the categories (widows, youth, elders, slaves, etc.) who made up the community and authorizing it to ward off those who endangered it (Tit. 3:10; 1:10-14; 1 Tim. 1:3; 4:7; 2 Tim. 2:25; 4:2). A discipline was imposed. It was this, as well as the proclamation and defense of the gospel so that the deposit of faith (*parathēkē*) should be kept and transmitted, which the charism (1 Tim. 4:14; 2 Tim. 1:6) made possible.

We thus come to a first conclusion. We see that the very roots of the ecclesial institution – the apostolic function and its derivatives – are in the strictest sense a gift of Christ to the church of God, given, guaranteed and supported by a *charisma* of the Holy Spirit. Thus it is not an adventitious phenomenon in the *oikonomia* of salvation but is integral to the gift of God. On the other hand, since the primary nucleus of the church of God was manifested at Pentecost as "apostolic", we can say that at the very moment of its "coming to light" the Spirit which constituted it as a *koinonia* gave it, along with the apostolate, the charisma that would also make of it the institution of salvation. It is not surprising that the book of Acts describes, in the stories of Ananias and Sapphira (5:1-11) and of the designation of the Seven (6:1-6), the first steps towards what would become the institution and the community discipline. Acts 15 shows how everything would quickly become theologically tied together: "the Holy Spirit and us" (v.28).[7] Moreover, beginning with Acts 14:21-27, we see the institution taking root.

It is thus impossible to cut the Spirit off from the institution, or, as is sometimes done even in Catholic theological circles, to distinguish sharply between what is from God (communion) and what is of human origin (the institution with all its avatars). The institution also has its roots in the divine gift. In the decisions of the Decree of Jerusalem are found all the conditions of a normative decree, proclaimed aloud and then communicated verbally and in writing. It is supported by the apostles and the elders in communion with the Spirit who has established them as *episkopoi* (guardians, overseers) of the churches (cf. 20:28).[8] The Spirit who guarantees the witness of the apostles (5:32) is the one who gives authority to this ministry of the elders in service to the *koinonia*. Without the Spirit, disciplinary decisions could not be imposed, above all in so grave a situation.

II

1. We may thus understand the ecclesiological and ecumenical importance of a few lines in which the Second Vatican Council's constitution *Lumen Gentium* reaffirms the sacramentality of the episcopacy, as well as those in which it emphasizes that the ministerial fullness, thus received, includes the charge of governing, along with the charges of sanctifying and teaching.

> And first, through the miraculous spokesmanship of the bishops, Christ addresses the word of God to all peoples and constantly administers the sacraments of the faith to believers; thanks to their paternal solicitude (cf. 1 Cor. 4:15) he incorporates new members into his Body by means of supernatural regeneration; and finally, through their wisdom and their prudence, he guides and prepares the people of the New Testament in its movement toward eternal blessedness. These shepherds, chosen to pasture the Lord's flock, are the ministers of Christ and the dispensers of the mysteries of God (cf. 1 Cor. 4:1); to them are entrusted the testimony rendered to the gospel of divine grace (cf. Rom. 15:16; Acts 20:24) and the glorious ministry of the Spirit and of justice (cf. 2 Cor. 3:8-9) (para. 21).

These ministers can accomplish all this only with the Spirit, whose power and assistance *ad hoc* are given sacramentally with the laying on of hands:

To fulfill so high a charge, the Apostles have been enriched by Christ with the treasures of the Holy Spirit, which descended upon them (cf. Acts 1:8; 2:4; John 20:22-23). Through the laying on of hands, they themselves confer this spiritual gift on their co-workers (cf. 1 Tim. 4:14; 2 Tim. 1:6-7), a gift which has been handed down to us in the episcopal consecration. The holy Council teaches, on the other hand, that this episcopal consecration confers the fulness of the sacrament of the order... Episcopal consecration confers, along with the charge of sanctification, also that of teaching and governing, though by their nature these charges can be exercised only in hierarchical communion with the Head and the members of the College. Indeed, from Tradition, as it arises especially from the liturgical rites and uses of the church, as much in the East as in the West, it emerges clearly that, through the laying on of hands and through the words of consecration, the grace of the Holy Spirit is conferred and the sacred character imprinted (para. 21).

Lumen Gentium also recalls that

the canonical mission of the bishops is handed on by means of legitimate customs not revoked by the supreme and universal authority of the Church, or by means of laws created or recognized by that same authority, or else directly by the successor of Peter himself; and if the latter refuses or denies apostolic communion, the bishops cannot enter upon their charges (para. 24).

Of the government of the local churches it is said:

The bishops govern the local churches entrusted to them in the quality of vicars and legates of Christ; they do so by their counsel, their persuasive words, their example, but also by authoritative decisions and by sacred power. They make use of this power, however, only to raise their flock in truth and godliness, recalling that whoever is greatest must make himself like the youngest, and the leader as one who serves (cf. Luke 22:26-27). This power which they exercise personally in the name of Christ is proper, ordinary and immediate, though the exercise of it is submitted in the last resort to the supreme authority of the Church and may be circumscribed within fixed limits, in consideration of the good of the Church or of the faithful. By virtue of this power, the bishops have the sacred right and, in the eyes of the Lord, the charge of legislating for their subjects, of judging and settling all that touches on the domain of worship and the apostolate (para. 27).

2. These last lines in particular make clear how the whole ecclesial institution – including the primacy of Rome, since the bishop of Rome is himself enrolled in the episcopal college of which he is the head – is built around the episcopacy, which comes from the Spirit sacramentally. This key point has not been sufficiently emphasized by the commentators on *Lumen Gentium*.

Indeed, the entire life of the church unfolds within the triple dynamism evoked by the three functions of preaching or instruction in the faith, celebration of the sacraments and the government of the local churches. It is the persons and groups charged with this triple activity, endowed with a juridical status which ensures its identity in all places and its maintenance in time, who constitute the axis of the ecclesial institution, the backbone of the visible ecclesial body upon which and in accordance with which other "institutions" (in the derivative and secondary sense specified above) are grafted.

This institution – and it alone – is essential to the structure of the church. Nothing can abolish it, because it comes precisely from the gift of God and is thus willed by God and destined to endure.[9] Through it, communion is accomplished and preserved in its essential nature. It is entirely caught up in the gift of the Spirit, since in each local church, in the provinces or regions, up to the level of catholicity as such, it is totally entrusted to the responsibility of the episcopal body, which exists only by the sacramental grace of the laying on of hands, thus by the Spirit. For the Catholic tradition, it is not indeed simply as persons that the bishops are *ad esse Ecclesiae*, but in so far as they are, through their ministry, the structural backbone, assuring the *diakonia* of Word, sacrament and discipline, which we call the institution. A lack of clarity on this point confuses discussions of the institution.

It is obvious that if the latter is a divine gift and thus a "spiritual" gift, it is all the same a gift incarnated in temporal realities. This gift becomes actual in a social and juridical apparatus whose elements are inseparable from all the complexity and heaviness of the human. The institution as conceived here is a divine gift that reaches persons and communities only in realities that are in essence properly human, not spiritual. They are as earthly as laws, regulations, groups of leaders, doctrines, rites – which can exist anywhere. Hence the complexity of the institution.

Let us say at once that the other "institutions" (in the derivative sense), which constitute either the setting required by circumstances of time and place or the means of sanctification in which the life of sacramental faith blossoms or manifestations of *koinonia*, are not essential. Nevertheless, they can engage the church only under the watchful eye of the institution (canons 113-23), being "received" by it. The case of the monastic or religious life is typical. The founding "charism" – which very often is manifested and takes shape without the intervention of the hierarchy – is not officially enfranchised until it is "received". All these "institutions" must obviously evolve, and some must even disappear if they no longer serve the *koinonia*. Otherwise they might disfigure the institution or make it sterile. What it comes down to – Vatican II was an illustration – is a purification by cutting off the dead branches of these "institutions".

3. The avatars of the institution are well known. But it is clear that we must distinguish between the essence of the institution and the forms it takes or the use to which it is put. At this point the human enters. To be sure, it may happen, particularly when exercising governing power or presenting the truth of the faith is involved, that the forms of exercising authority become oppressive because they do not really take account of the dignity of persons. Those in responsibility may fail to adapt their directives to new situations. Out of fear or because of a misinterpretation of people's real intentions, the holders of the difficult mission of preserving ecclesial teaching and doctrine may block research when an intuition precious for the future is germinating. The "evangelical mystique of service" may slowly turn into a bureaucracy or suffer administrative sclerosis or contract the gangrene of politics. These are risks and blunders which nourish suspicion of and sometimes even repulsion towards the institution. It secretes its own ills and thus engenders its enemies.

However, the same point applies here as Augustine (later seconded by Thomas Aquinas) vigorously maintained during the turmoil of the Donatist crisis. The poverty of the minister – which obviously does not have the same role here as in the sacrament – must not be confused with the institution to the extent of leading to the negation of the relation of the latter with the Spirit. Recall Augustine's fury against "bad shepherds". Precisely by their fault, the "grace" of the institution was veiled, compromised. He accuses them of perverting the gift which God never ceases to offer so that the ministerial institution may remain a servant of communion.[10] It is not the institution as such that must be incriminated, but those who make it deviate from its authentic faith. The structure of the institution remains; "institutions" and modes of exercise must evolve so that the community may be spared the deterioration of life-in-communion.

III

1. But the church of God is not only the institution. Moreover, since Vatican II, the custom of identifying the church with the hierarchical apparatus, its official face, is slowly disappearing, even in the media. For the church of God is also and above all the community which the institution forms, preserves, nourishes spiritually, stabilizes, perpetuates in time and space. It is the *koinonia* of the faithful with the Father and among themselves, through the Son, in the Spirit. Here once again it is impossible to cut off the institution from the community in communion. On the one hand, the members of the former belong to the latter and thus, as such, are also beneficiaries of the institution itself and subject to the risks that lie in wait for it. In the church of God, no one can escape from the institution, precisely because it is a gift of God for all. On the other hand, and this is the essential point, the same Holy Spirit is at work both in all the faithful of the community and in the institution, towards the same end. The Spirit invoked in the baptismal epiclesis and the eucharistic epiclesis, who makes of these two sacraments the visible manifestation of the church, is also the one who welds together the members of the *koinonia*. The action of the Spirit through the channels of the institution and the action of the Spirit in people's hearts are, says scholasticism, the two faces of the same mission of the Spirit – two faces in constant osmosis.

2. Here we come to the *sensus fidelium* and its role in the health – and sometimes healing – of the institution, drawing it out of sclerosis and a sterile attachment to lazy conformity. Understanding this role is essential to understanding the relation between the Spirit and the institution.

Several times Augustine rejects the granting of a monopoly on sacerdotal dignity to the body of bishops and those who constitute the institution as we define it.[11] For the title of *sacerdos* belongs to the whole of the Christian community, incorporated under Christ the Priest. It is moreover by virtue of this title that the whole assembly is associated with the bishop, with the *presbyterium*, with the entire ministerial company in the celebration and offering of the eucharist. In its relation to the Spirit, despite the diversity of functions demanded by its life as the Body of Christ, the church of God is not divided in what comes to it from Christ by the Spirit. It is "one in the Spirit and in Christ". All, without exclusivity and without exception, are integrated by the Spirit into a single sacerdotal Body of Christ, in which all commune in grace. Augustine goes so far as to affirm: "Once [in the Old Testament] the priest alone was anointed, now all Christians receive unction."[12] The entire church *as such* participates in the royal and sacerdotal quality of its Head. Not only the *praepositus* but "the rest of the Body is the body of the Priest"[13] and the body of the Lord, taking part in the lordly and sacerdotal ecclesial reality in what is most essential to it. That is why, between those who are part of the institution, through the Spirit who makes them gifts of Christ to the church, and the community as a whole, there is not merely unilateral communication but interrelation. The institution is never independent of the *sensus fidelium*. The latter is its safeguard. That holds not only for the sacramental (sacerdotal) and prophetic register but also for the "royal" register.

The notion of the *sensus fidei* and *sensus fidelium* has been refined in recent years.[14] The impact of the *sensus fidei* is no longer limited (as Newman seems to limit it)[15] to the register of doctrinal questions. Reflection on both the liturgical movement and liturgical participation has made it possible to deepen and give a dogmatic foundation on the one hand to the influence of the *vota* of the whole community, laypersons included, and on the other hand to the ecclesiological significance of the participation of all (according to their *charisma*) in the single and indivisible sacramental *synaxis* of the local church *as such*. Especially since the *Mediator Dei* (20 November 1947) of Pius XII and the Congress of Assisi in 1956, the questioning of the institution by the *sensus fidei*, which has its source in the Spirit, has been evident.[16] The institution has thus gradually and prudently opened itself to a new dynamism, the bearers of which were for the most part monks and nuns, laypersons, Catholic action movements and scouts. There has been a "reception" (in the strong sense of the word) by the institution of those desires of the Spirit expressed in what Augustine called the sacerdotal and royal body as a whole.

In addition, what is known as "the participation of the faithful in the sacramental act" is henceforth understood in all its "sacerdotal" density. Not a simple acquiescence to the minister's act and a simple "perception" of the *res* of the sacrament, but a true *communion* in all that is accomplished. Often there is grafted on to it the type of cooperation which is praised (with a warning against deviations) by the Roman Instruction of 13 August 1997 on "Several Questions Concerning the Collaboration of the Lay Faithful in the Ministry of the Priests". Preparation for baptism and marriage, readings, monitions, music, singing, general prayer and if need be the distribution of communion are falling more and more to laypersons. By "receiving" these activities and integrating them into the full liturgy, the institution "receives" the desire of the Spirit for a living church, in communion with humanity. To be convinced of this, one need only spend a Holy Week in Kinshasa when Cardinal Malula presides over the Liturgy. There it is clear that to "collaborate" means neither to "substitute" nor to efface oneself.

But this holds equally for the register of government. The exhortation *Christi fideles laici* (1988) urged responsible members of the institution to "recognize" the offices and functions of the non-ordained faithful, in order to promote them. Furthermore, canon law (canons 517, 230, 861, 1112) provides for "deputed lay ministries" in addition to the "instituted ministries" of acolyte and reader, for functions to be performed in the name of the institution, *in persona Ecclesiæ*.[17] Here we are neither in the realm of the ecclesial "services" which any baptized person may be called on to render according to the circumstances, some of which are essential to the life of the local church (catechism, liturgical assistance, missionary work, preparation for the sacraments, financial administration, legal assistance; canon 228); nor in the immense field of activity of the members of religious orders who are not clerics, above all in health, education and care for the poor. In the case that concerns us, it is rather a question of charges which by their nature ought to be carried out by ordained ministers, as the only ones responsible for them. But the shortage of the latter has led to their being entrusted to laymen deputed for the purpose.

The code of 1983 is explicit (it is useful to quote it for non-Catholic readers, since it is often ignored):

> If, owing to the shortage of priests, the diocesan bishop believes he must entrust to a deacon or other person not vested with sacerdotal character, or else to a community of persons, a participation in the exercise of the pastoral charge of a parish, he shall appoint a priest who, provided with the powers and capacities of a curate, will be the moderator of the pastoral charge (canon 517:2).

We are well within the domain of the institution. Moreover, it is said in reference to more precise cases:

> Where the need of the Church demands it, for lack of ministers, laymen, even if they are not readers or acolytes, may also fill certain of their functions – namely, to exercise the ministry of the word, to preside over liturgical prayers, confer baptism and distribute holy communion, according to the dispositions of the law (canon 230:3; see canon 861).
>
> Where there is neither priest nor deacon, the diocesan bishop, on the favourable opinion of the conference of bishops and with the authorization of the Holy See, may delegate laymen to assist at marriages. He must choose a competent layman, capable of giving instruction to the future couple and able to perform the marriage liturgy properly (canon 1112).

These cases and provisions are certainly not changing the nature of institutional ministry. They are justified only by the desire not to create a pastoral void in communities without an "ordained minister". The laymen in question have no pastoral charge. Yet they participate in the exercise of a pastoral charge, by means of an official deputation which puts them in communion with the responsibility of those upon whom the institution rests. For, in the ministerial team provided for by canon 517:2, they have a status quite different from that of the members of the "pastoral council" (canon 536). They find themselves inserted into the very dynamism of the pastoral act, the intra-ecclesial source of which can only be the ordained minister. Indeed, this source is necessarily sacramental, linked with Christ the Head and the apostolic community. Only sacramental ordination "consecrates and deputes" (canon 1008) for ecclesial acts performed "*in persona Christi capitis*".

Laymen, while remaining such, are thus deputed by the bishop to a pastoral charge which is inscribed, without ordination, in a necessary *communion* with the ordained minister – founded on this explicit, official delegation from the bishop – and by virtue of which they perform authentically pastoral acts. They are in some way grafted onto the institution, though without truly being members of it. On the basis of their baptismal sacerdocy, the institution deputes them to assume precise, delicate and important functions which would normally be incumbent on itself. As we see, on this register which is doubtless most typical of the institution, the shortcomings and impoverishments of the latter are, by virtue of the common grace of the Spirit, as if "supplied", "made up for" in the people of God by exceptional enlistments of laymen. In this case, with the sole power of the Spirit received at baptism, the goal normally attained by the institution is realized, though it be in need, because laymen of the community come to its aid. Without this aid, it would waste away, breathless, without success, and the wound would be borne by the whole church. It should be stressed that the laymen thus "deputized" are not mere executors of orders coming from elsewhere. They are engaged with all their Christian responsibility of heeding the Spirit, their generosity, and in certain circumstances the capacity for initiative given them by their *sensus fidei*.

The same is true, moreover, for all the lay members of various diocesan or parochial councils (canons 492, 512, 536, 537), the members of diocesan synods (canon 460), of their function as diocesan judges (canon 1421), case examiners (canon 1428), defenders of the marriage bond (canons 1434-36), assessors (canon 1424), promoters of justice (canons 1434-36), chancellors (according to the current interpretation of canon 483:2) and professors of theology. These are all functions arising from the very mission of the institution, and into which laymen are integrated with their own judgment and *prudentia* as baptized persons guided by the Spirit from whom they take their *sensus fidei*. These new canonical decisions, sometimes required by the necessities of our times, help us to understand the real nature and scope of the institution and its relation to the whole community.

But it is also within the complex domain of fidelity to the truth and to the doctrine of faith that this interaction of the institution and the *sensus fidei* is verified. Since this point has been examined many times, we shall not linger over it. In so far as they belong to the Body of Christ and try to live in conformity with his Spirit, following what Augustine calls the inner Master, Christians acquire a sort of instinct that comes from this Spirit. The same Holy Spirit that dwelt in Jesus and with whom the apostolic Pentecostal community was filled (Acts 2:4; 4:31; 7:55) "abides" in the whole Body.

In this the Spirit fulfills the mission of communicating the good of Christ, causing the words and gestures of the Lord to be "remembered" specifying their meaning in accordance with different situations and needs. He acts within the ecclesial Body, in its members. He creates in them a sort of profound accord, an instinctive harmony with the Truth, an evangelical scent, a spiritual ear. Just as a friend grasps that a certain word or attitude is a betrayal of friendship, so the Christian truly integrated into the Body of Christ will feel as if by instinct that a certain declaration or a certain way of doing things is a betrayal of Christ. Just as a person with a musical ear is spontaneously able to discover an off-key voice in the choir, so the Christian inhabited by the Spirit perceives that a certain custom, once perhaps legitimate, or a certain opinion or interpretation henceforth clashes with communion in the Body of Christ.

The new code of canon law provides "institutions" for the expression of this *sensus fidei*, either personally or in the experience of a synod, thus attesting that the church lives from the truth perceived through this *sensus fidei*. The Spirit makes Christ speak, as it were, in his members, inscribed in their various geographical and historical contexts. While remaining the same, his voice is diversified according to times and cultures, the word of salvation for the whole of humanity.

Thus if the church of God is not stagnant, if in the course of time it continues to be in communion with the aspirations, sufferings and intuitions of humanity carried along in the movement of history, it is owing to this *sensus fidei* of genuine Christians. More often it is they more than the members of the hierarchy who keep pushing the church further ahead, urging it to espouse the evolution of cultural dynamisms. It is also they who enroll it in a realistic communion with the human condition. For they bear in their flesh both the dramas and the joys of concrete existence. The Spirit teaches them that their tears and sufferings are not foreign to Christ and must thus be a concern of the church. If the church has always wished to be in the service of God's compassion, that is without doubt because the Spirit has opened the eyes of the heart of many Christians, above all laypersons, to the sting of human misery. They have thus evangelized the institution. Indeed, those who have responsibility for the latter "receive" these manifestations so that, weighed with the discernment of the same Spirit that puts them in his service, they may be guided in their presentation or interpretation of doctrine and in their decision-making.

What would the Second Vatican Council have been if the assembled bishops had not thus "received" what the Spirit had brought forth from the desires, the disturbances, the plans, the discomforts, the timid initiatives in the Body of Christ? What would have happened if they had refused all that had been born outside the hierarchy? They would have "quenched the Spirit" (1 Thess. 5:19). The Spirit does not let himself be domesticated and dominated by the institution. At the very heart of the church the Spirit is able, if necessary, to impose his authority on it through the faithful themselves. Thus, by the symbiosis of the "charismatic" and the institutional, he makes the Body of Christ live. He makes of it at once a reality of God and of humanity that lives only in history.

3. That said, we must emphasize also that without the institution the *sensus fidei* would be unable to come to full maturity. Indeed we might say that it is the consequence of the presence of the Spirit in the baptized. But it exists in them in so far as they participate in the profound reality of the ecclesial Body *as such*. If they were not in communion with it, they would not have this *sensus fidei*. For it is to this communion that it is formally granted. It is, in each living member, the actualization of the *instinctus*, of the *sensus*, of the whole body joined to its Head and inhabited by the Spirit. For to the mission of the Spirit belong the "remembrance" of the *acta et dicta* of Jesus Christ and the communication of the gifts with which he fills the Risen Lord for the sake of humankind. Since there is no Christ without the church, as there is no head without a body, so the Spirit "plenishes" (*plēroō*) Christ, by giving him an ecclesial Body, living from him and his salvation.[18] In each of the baptized, whom faithfulness to the gospel brings existentially into union with Christ, the Spirit thus gives expression to the consciousness of the Body of Christ, in accordance with new needs and contexts, upbuilding itself in the world until he comes (1 Cor. 11:26).

But we have shown, basing ourselves above all on the letter to the Ephesians, that it was precisely the function of the institution to build, with the power of the Spirit, the Body of Christ and to preserve it in its communion. It is the gift, through the Spirit, of the structure around which the *koinonia* constructs itself, articulates itself, preserves itself and propagates itself in word, sacrament and discipline of the new life. Without it, there would be no constant and articulated proclamation of the authentic content of the revelation, no sacrament of baptism or eucharist, no law of personal and community life according to the gospel. Thus there would be no matter for any "remembrance", for any participation in the *instinctus* of the Body, since the latter would not exist, constructed "upon the foundation of the apostles and prophets" (Eph. 2:20; cf. 3:4; 4:11), who are the guarantors, inseparable from "the time that the Lord Jesus went in and out among us", and "witnesses to his resurrection" (Acts 1:21-22), of the bond with Israel. The institution needs the *sensus fidei,* but this *sensus fidei* exists and is expressed in the work of the institution. Each has need of the other.

IV

1. As a contribution to this study of *episkopé,* we have proposed to show the bond between the institution, as we have defined it, starting from indications to be found especially in the letter to the Ephesians and the pastoral epistles, and the Holy Spirit. We have distinguished three essential points. (1) The institution has appeared to us as a gift of the Spirit for the *koinonia* of the Body of Christ, a gift always at risk because of the weakness of human agents, a gift nevertheless always inscribed in the normal *oikonomia* of salvation. (2) Always on the basis of the *gratia* granted in the faith and the sacraments of the faith, the Holy Spirit enables the faithful bearers of the *sensus fidei* to correct, heal, enlighten, adapt the institution, and even to make up for its failings. (3) All the same, this *sensus fidei* remains dependent on the institution in its fundamental registers, since it is given only in the Body of Christ, for the building, preservation and maintenance of which the institution is the Spirit's instrument. In the church of God there is thus an interaction in both directions, between the "servants of the Spirit" and the community of the "temple of the Spirit" (1 Cor. 6:19; Eph. 2:21-22). The presence of the Spirit and his ecclesial work are connected with this interaction.

It is clear, then, that the institution should not be considered a purely human element, foreign to the essence of the work of the Spirit. It belongs to the *oikonomia* of grace.

This place of the institution obviously does not conceal the fact that the Spirit transcends it, that institutional and canonical frontiers do not exactly cover the field of the Spirit's action. The Spirit who acted in humanity before the birth of Christ now acts in humanity outside the institution, in unsuspected ways. He is in no way the slave of the institution. He is its master.

It may also happen that the responsible members of the institution hardly welcome this action of the Spirit even within the church, when it upsets its too-easy attainments, contests its conformism, denounces its errors. The Dominican figures of Savonarola, of Bartolomé de las Casas, of Père Lagrange, of a whole generation of researchers who preceded and prepared for Vatican II, are known to us. Their thought and their witness passed through a long purgatory before being "received". They were resisted. Sometimes this resistance ended in tragedy. Thus some of the great fractures that continue to break up the unity of the people of God have their origin in this resistance of the institution. Here the excuses of Paul VI and John Paul II find their ecclesiological significance.

As for the influence of the saints, it rarely coincides with the institution, unless the latter integrates them into liturgical worship. They are, indeed, like all Christians, in need of the means of grace the institution provides. They cannot live without the institution. However, above all in our contemporary societies, it is they, far more than the institution, who witness to the Spirit. Their witness calls out both to other Christians and to unbelievers. Moreover, the monasteries and contemplative communities have for centuries remained the relay-stations for a presence of the Spirit who takes paths other than those of the institution to give life to the church of God. It is highly significant that in times of crisis it is usually the monasteries that are asked to supply bishops, and that in the West the prayer of the monks has been the inspiration for the great liturgical prayer of all the people of God. The institution knows how to be a mendicant.

* * *

Once again the wise old axiom is verified: not *either... or* but *both... and.* The Spirit and the institution together make the church of God, and in this togetherness the Spirit has full mastery. But all the same, God himself wants this institution.

Translated from the French
by Richard Pevear

NOTES

[1] *Sermo* 223,2, *PL* 38, 1092-1093; *BA* 72, p.833. Cf. *De doct. Christ* 3, 22, 45, *BA* 11, p.400; *Tract. In Joh.* 6, 2, *BA* 71, p.346; *Tract. In Joh.* 27, 11, *BA* 72, p.561; *Tract. In Joh.* 7, 1, *BA* 7, p.404; *Tract. In Joh.* 28, 11, *BA* 72, p.595; *Contra epist. Parm.* 3, 3, 19, *BA* 28, pp.440-42; *Contra Faust.* 12, 15, *PL* 42, pp.262-63; *Sermo* 111, 3 (ed. Lambot, RB 1947, 115).

[2] The church "must bear in mind that among these very enemies are hidden her future citizens... In the same way, while the City of God is on pilgrimage in this world, she has in her midst some who are united with her in participation in the sacraments, but who will not join with her in the eternal destiny of the saints... But, such as they are, we have less right to despair of the reformation of some of them, when some predestined friends, as yet unknown even to themselves, are concealed among our most open enemies. In truth, those two cities are interwoven and intermixed in this era, and await separation at the last judgment" (*De civ. Dei,* 1, 35; *BA* 33, pp.298-300). "According to the foreknowledge of him who knows those whom *he has predestined before the creation of the world to be conformed to the image of his Son* (Rom. 8:29 and Eph. 1:4), many of those who are openly outside and are called heretics are better than many good Catholics; what they are today, we see; what they will be tomorrow, we do not know, but clearly for God, before whom the future is already present, they are even now what they will be tomorrow" (*De bapt.,* 4, 3, 4; *BA* 29, p.240). "There are some who are still living in iniquity or who have even fallen into heresies or into the superstitions of the pagans, and yet even there *the Lord knows those who are his* (2 Tim. 2:19), for in this ineffable foreknowledge of God many of those who seem to be outside are inside and many of those who seem to be inside are outside" (*De bapt.* 5, 27, 38; *BA* 29, p.396). "According to the foreknowledge of God, just as many sheep have wandered outside, so many wolves lie in ambush within; among them, however, *the Lord knows those who are his*: he knows those who will be left for the fire; he knows the wheat on his threshing floor and he knows the straw; he knows the harvest and he knows the tares" (*Tract. In Joh.,* 12, 12; *BA* 71, p.659; cf. *Contra epist. Parm.,* 2, 11, 25; *De bapt.,* 5, 28, 39; *Contra litt. Petil.,* 3, 3, 4; *BA* 28, p. 335; 29, p.400; 30, pp. 590-92). It is love that makes the division between the two cities (*De civ. Dei* 14, 28; *BA* 35, p.464), and "God alone can judge, he who knows the secrets of the heart" (*En. In Ps.,* 43; *PL* 36, 491). "The just and the unjust have indeed the same aspect; both are men, but both are not mansions of God, even if each is called Christian" (*Sermo* 15, 2; *CC* 41, p.194). "Many sheep wander outside... He alone knows by his predestination and foreknowledge the sheep and the goats who was able to predestine and know

in advance" (*Sermo* 47, 16 and 15; *ibid.* p.585). "You must think that every man is your neighbour, even before he becomes a Christian, for you do not know what he is to God, you are ignorant of how God knows him in his foreknowledge... We who do not know the future must hold every man to be our neighbour, not only by the condition of his human mortality, but also by the hope of eternal inheritance" (*En. In Ps.* 25, en. 2, 2; *PL* 36, 189). "He of whom we despaired was converted and became very good; he of whom we presumed so much began to weaken and became very bad" (*Sermo* 46, 27; *CC* 41, p.553). The church thus cannot keep itself to religious categories that divide people into Christians, Jews and pagans, but must entrust itself, with all the optimism of its hope, to the almightiness of him who is able to transform the worshippers of idols into children of Abraham (*Sermo* 24, 2, citing Matt. 3:9; *CC* 41, p.527). Cf. P. Borgomeo, *L'Église de ce temps dans la prédication de saint Augustin*, Paris, 1972, pp.279-356; and M. F. Berrouard, note 9, in *BA* 73B, pp.430-433, which we have followed.

[3] See Michel Bouttier, *L'épitre de saint Paul aux Ephésiens*, Geneva, 1991, pp.185-98. On this text we follow the interpretation of J.N. Collins, *Diakonia, Re-interpreting the Ancient Sources*, New York, 1990.

[4] M. Bouttier, *op. cit.*, pp.185f.

[5] *Ibid.*, p.187.

[6] See R. Schnackenberg, *The Epistle to the Ephesians*, Edinburgh, 1991, pp.184-86.

[7] In the words of E. Haenchen, *The Acts of the Apostles*, London, 1971, p.453, "the highest supernatural authority and the legal earthly authority derived from it stand side by side". Compare 15:28 with 5:32.

[8] See M. Simon, "The Apostolic Decree and its Setting in the Ancient Church", *Bulletin of the John Rylands Library*, Vol. 52, 1969-70, pp.437-60; Ch. Perrot, "La tradition apostolique dans les Actes des Apôtres", *L'Année canonique*, Vol. 23, 1979, pp.25-35; D.R. Catchpole, "Paul, James and the Apostolic Decree", *NTS*, Vol. 23, 1976-77, pp.428-44.

[9] See J.M.R. Tillard, *Église d'Églises*, Paris, 1987, p.380.

[10] See in particular *Sermo* 46, *CCSL* 41, 535-57.

[11] Above all the sermon known as "Dolbeau 26"; see G. Rémy, "Le Christ Médiateur et Tête de l'Église, selon le Sermon Dolbeau 26 d'Augustin", *Revue des Sciences Religieuses*, Vol. 72, 1998, pp.3-19; Augustin, *Vingt-six Sermons au Peuple d'Afrique*, collection of *Études August.*, 147, Paris, 1996, pp.345-441.

[12] *Ibid.*, no. 50, 1211-12 (F. Dolbeau, *Vingt-six Sermons au Peuple d'Afrique*, p.405). This is the context: "*Universa tamen ecclesia corpus est illius sacerdotis. Ad sacerdotem pertinet corpus suum. Nam et apostolus Petrus ideo dicit ad ipsam ecclesiam: 'Plebs sancta, regale sacerdotium'. [50]. Tunc unus sacerdos ungebatur, modo christiani omnes unguntur. Ungebatur rex, ungebatur sacerdos, ceteri non ungebantur. Utramque personam gerebat dominus, non in figura, sed iam in veritate, et regis et sacerdotis.*" See also *Contra ep. Parmeniani*, II, VII-VIII, *BA* 28.

[13] *Ibid.*, no. 53, 1295.

[14] See J. Burkhard, "*Sensus fidei*: Theological Reflection since Vatican II: 1. 1965-1985, 2. 1985-1989," in *The Heythrop Journal*, Vol. 34, 1993, pp.41-59, 123-36; J.M.R. Tillard, "L'Église locale", in *Cogitatio fidei*, no. 191, Paris, 1995, pp.314-33.

[15] "On Consulting the Faithful in Matters of Doctrine", in *The Rambler*, 1859, pp.219-23, reprinted by J. Coulson, Kansas City, 1961.

[16] See A. Bugnini, "Documenta Pontificia ad Instaurationem liturgicam spectantia (1903-1953)", in *Bibl. Ephem. lit.*, no. 6, Rome, 1953, p.47.

[17] See J.M.R. Tillard, *L'Église locale*, pp.214-19; the expression "recognized and trusted ministers" does not seem to me precise enough. On this see also *La Maison-Dieu*, no. 194, 1993, especially the articles by Paul de Clerck, "Des laïcs ministres des sacrements?" (pp.27-45); P. Gy, "La

célébration du baptême, du mariage et des funerailles confiée à des laïcs" (pp.14-25); and P. Valdrini, "Fonction de sanctification et charge pastorale" (pp.47-58); cf. also A. van der Helm, *Un clergé parallèle*, Strasbourg, CERDIC, 1994; B. Sesboüé, "Les Animateurs pastoraux laïcs. Une prospective théologique", *Études,* no. 337, 1992, pp.253-69.

[18] The Johannine text most often invoked as the basis of this *sensus fidei* (1 John 2:20-27) supports this reading. See I. de la Potterie, "La Vie selon l'Esprit", *Una Sancta*, Vol. 55, 1965, pp.85-105, 126-44; and M.-E. Boismard, "La connaissance dans l'Alliance Nouvelle d'après la première lettre de S. Jean," *Revue biblique*, Vol. 56, 1949, pp.364-91.

2. *EPISKOPÉ* AND EPISCOPACY: ORTHODOX PERSPECTIVES

John H. Erickson

The preferred way of approaching theological issues in the East has been described as circular and contemplative, in contrast to the linear and analytical approach of the West. Representative figures like Maximus the Confessor and Gregory Palamas introduce one aspect of the mystery under consideration, often in the form of pithy maxims drawn from the fathers who went before them; then, without fully developing it, they move on to other aspects, only to return to the initial aspects at a later point, this time from a higher, broader perspective. Theology thus becomes an ascending spiral which circles around the mystery without ever exhausting it. In the observations which follow, I shall adopt this Eastern approach, though whether the figure traced will be an ascending or a descending spiral I cannot guarantee.

In a survey of the contributions of recent Orthodox-Catholic dialogue to the subject of *episkopé* and episcopacy, the most obvious sources requiring comment include:

- The 1988 "Valamo Statement" of the Joint International Commission for Theological Dialogue between the Catholic and Orthodox Churches ("The Sacrament of Order in the Sacramental Structure of the Church with Particular Reference to the Importance of Apostolic Succession for the Sanctification and Unity of the People of God"), along with portions of the Joint International Commission's 1982 "Munich Statement" ("The Mystery of the Church and of the Eucharist in the Light of the Mystery of the Holy Trinity").[1]
- Responses of the US Orthodox-Catholic Theological Consultation to the "Valamo Statement" and the "Munich Statement", issued in 1989 and 1983 respectively.[2]
- Other statements of the US Orthodox-Catholic Consultation, including "The Pastoral Office" (1976); "An Agreed Statement on the Lima Document: *Baptism, Eucharist and Ministry*" (1984); "Apostolicity as God's Gift in the Life of the Church" (1986); "An Agreed Statement on Conciliarity and Primacy in the Church" (1989).[3]

Most of these texts date from the 1980s. They are "recent" only in the sense that Orthodox-Catholic dialogue has contributed very little to the subject of *episkopé* since then. After meeting in Valamo in 1988, the Joint International Commission had been expected to meet next in Munich in 1990 to prepare a statement on "Ecclesiological and Canonical Consequences of the Sacramental Structures of the Church: Conciliarity and Authority in the Church". By then, however, in the wake of the collapse of communism in Eastern Europe, this dialogue faced new challenges. Discussion turned from relatively abstract issues of ecclesiology to practical issues relating to "uniatism" and proselytism.

But to describe even the 1988 Valamo Statement as "recent" may be misleading. Some sections consist simply of quotations from the 1982 Munich Statement (paras 46-48 quote Munich II.4 and III.4). Even greater portions of the text, as well as its basic structure, are taken from the "Orthodox-Roman Catholic Reflections on Ministries" published in 1977 on the basis of still earlier discussions.[4] The main Orthodox contributor both to these "Reflections" and to the work of the Joint International Commission, as well as to *BEM*, was Metropolitan John Zizioulas, whose published articles from this period also touch on many aspects of *episkopé* and episcopacy.[5] While it would be no exaggeration to say that Zizioulas has provided the most recent Orthodox contribution to the discussion of *episkopé* and episcopacy, he is simply the most recent – if most brilliant – of the Orthodox exponents of the "eucharistic ecclesiology" pioneered by Nicholas Afanasiev; and like Afanasiev and his heirs Zizioulas appeals repeatedly in support of his position to the witness of the fathers, above all to the ante-Nicene fathers. Inevitably, therefore, discussion of the most "recent" Orthodox-Catholic statements on *episkopé* and episcopacy leads us back to the ecclesiology of the first centuries of the church.

There are two reasons why modern Orthodox presentations relating to *episkopé* and episcopacy have concentrated on the period between the New Testament and the Council of Nicea. First, it is argued that this period provides an important, indeed normative, point of reference for ecclesiology and theological reflection. As Zizioulas puts it, "It is not any idea of the bishop but that of the ancient church that I regard as normative for the Orthodox doctrine."[6] Second, the pattern of episcopacy in this period – subsequent to the unique and unreproducible apostolic age but prior to the establishment of Christianity as a state religion under Constantine – may be of particular relevance in our own post-apostolic but also post-Constantinian age. Among other things, it may be more acceptable to non-episcopal communities than the Constantinian-era pattern which determined the course of the 16th-century debates between Protestants and Catholics.[7]

Within this period, three main aspects of episcopal ministry have been discerned. Each can conveniently be associated with a particular church father: Ignatius of Antioch, Irenaeus of Lyons and Cyprian of Carthage.

- For Ignatius, the bishop is above all the president of the local eucharistic assembly. It is he who gathers the diverse gifts of the local community into unity, as they become one body of Christ through participation in the one eucharistic loaf. He is an *alter Christus*, a living icon who constitutes "the focus and visible centre of unity within the church",[8] who expresses "the fullness, unity and multiplicity of the eschatological community in each place".[9]

– For Irenaeus the bishop is above all an authoritative teacher and witness to the apostolic faith, an *alter apostolus*. His outward continuity in succession back to the apostles through his predecessors in the same see "serves as the sign and guarantee of inward continuity in apostolic faith".[10] Thus he is a living link between his local church and the apostles. He expresses "the historical continuity of the church in time"[11] – a continuity not merely of structures but of apostolic faith.

– For Cyprian, the bishop is part of a worldwide episcopal college, co-responsible with his brother bishops for maintaining the unity and good estate of all the churches. An *alter Petrus*, he expresses "the communion and unity of the church in space".[12] He is therefore a conciliar being. He possesses the fullness of episcopal grace not in isolation but in union with all the other bishops, and he serves as the bond of unity between his own local church and all the other local churches.

How can these three images of *episkopé* be held together in a coherent synthesis, so that the Irenaean ministry of the word is organically joined to the Ignatian ministry of sacrament and not simply parallel to it, so that the Cyprianic ministry of wider oversight is organically joined to both and not simply an external administrative office? This question has been important for the internal life of the churches at several points in their history, especially at times of division and conflict. Today it is significant as the churches strive for reconciliation and mutual recognition of ministries. Whether tacitly or explicitly, the churches and the major Christian traditions they represent have acknowledged the importance of all three perspectives, but they have brought them together in different ways, sometimes employing differing organizing principles, sometimes emphasizing elements that other traditions have neglected or subordinated. At the risk of oversimplification, let me offer some very broad characterizations of how the Ignatian, Irenaean and Cyprianic images of *episkopé* have been employed by Orthodox, Protestants and Catholics.

If one were to correlate these early fathers with modern confessional emphases, one might argue that magisterial Protestantism has tended to look to Irenaeus for its inspiration and orientation. Though not preoccupied with certain aspects of historical continuity, such as the maintenance of institutional forms, it has strongly emphasized the role of the ordained ministry in witness to and proclamation of the apostolic faith, on the basis of apostolic scripture. While perhaps willing to acknowledge continuity in the apostolic succession of bishops as an important *sign* of continuity in apostolic faith, Protestants have generally been unwilling to see it as a *guarantee* of faith. Indeed, at the time of the Reformation they were willing to abandon the "historic episcopate" to the extent that this was experienced as an obstacle to apostolic preaching and faith. Certainly they would reject the tendency in some older presentations of Catholic sacramental theology to look on apostolic succession above all as mechanism for ensuring the preservation of "valid" sacraments, to the point of detaching it from broader aspects of the life and faith of the church community.

Here we may note a certain affinity with the Orthodox. Often to the bewilderment and annoyance of their ecumenical partners, the Orthodox have insisted that mutual recognition of sacraments and ministry is inseparable from mutual recognition of faith. Recognition depends not just on agreement about the subject immediately under consideration (e.g. eucharistic doctrine) but on agreement about the faith in its totality. Thus it is not so surprising that the Bari Statement (1987) of the Catholic-Orthodox Joint International Commission stopped well short of the mutual recognition of baptism that some had been expecting, or that its Valamo Statement (1988) stopped short of mutual recognition of ministry, even though there would appear to be no substantial differences between the churches on either subject.

Roman Catholic presentations of ecclesiology have historically taken their cue from Cyprian's dictum *episcopates unus est*. Their point of departure has been the unity of episcopate as a collective body, a single college having as its single head the veritable successor of Peter. While Catholic theologians like Tillard, Legrand and Komonchak have adopted many elements of the Ignatian perspective, relating the ministry of the bishop to the life and faith of the local church, they have done so in the face of an ecclesiological tradition which has tended to value universality over diversity and particularity.

The continuing strength of the Cyprianic perspective is evident, for example, in the *Communionis notio* of the Congregation for the Doctrine of the Faith, which argues for the priority of the universal over the local, as well as the *Codex Iuris Canonici* (1983) and the *Codex Canonum Ecclesiarum Orientalium* (1990), which are far more concerned with issues of episcopal collegiality (especially the relationship between primacy and episcopacy) than with the place of the bishop within the communion of his local church.[13] Archbishop Rembert G. Weakland, Catholic co-chairman of the US Catholic-Orthodox Theological Consultation, has observed:

> We Roman Catholics use the phrase "Universal Church" more often than we realize. It is a phrase that most characterizes our ecclesiological position... Especially since Vatican II, we have evolved an elaborate thinking on how the universal church is present in the local church and realized there. We Roman Catholics almost always begin with such universalism and then proceed to local manifestations... The Orthodox begin with the local church and the celebration of the eucharist on the local level. The local eucharistic community – rather than the concept of a universal church – is their starting point.[14]

While this characterization of Roman Catholicism seems to me to be on target, I believe the characterization of Orthodoxy requires some qualification. Certain there have been periods in Orthodox church history when a universal, "Cyprianic" perspective has been present in significant ways. While episcopal conciliarity has usually been emphasized more than primacy, some rather papal-sounding statements can be found which call attention to the role of the ecumenical patriarch as head of a universal episcopate, responsible for shepherding the church understood as a universal organism. Towards the end of the Byzantine period, for example, Patriarch Philotheus Coccinus spoke of himself as "leader of all Christians found anywhere in the *oikoumene*", "protector and guardian of their souls", "the father and teacher of them all", who, because he cannot physically be present everywhere, "chooses the best among men, the most eminent in virtue, establishes and ordains them as pastors, teachers and high priests, and sends them to the end of the universe... so that each, in the country and place appointed him, enjoys territorial rights, and episcopal see, and all the rights of Our Humility".[15]

Over the centuries, Irenaean and Cyprianic elements have never been entirely absent from Orthodox practice and reflection. But they certainly have been overshadowed in modern Orthodox presentations of ecclesiology by the Ignatian image of the local eucharistic community. Afanasiev, for example, goes so far as to oppose the "eucharistic ecclesiology" of Ignatius to other approaches, most notably to the "universal ecclesiology" of Cyprian. Others have been more nuanced. Zizioulas, for example, sees in Hippolytus' *Apostolic Tradition* a synthesis between the iconic approach of Ignatius and the historical approach of I Clement and Irenaeus.[16] So also, in contrast to Afanasiev, he tries to hold together the approaches of Ignatius and Cyprian, insisting that "the nature of the eucharist points not in the direction of the priority of the local church but in that of the *simultaneity* of both local and universal".[17] Still, as this statement suggests, his point of departure remains the eucharist as revealed in the letter of Ignatius, the *Didaché* and other early Christian texts.

While modern eucharistic ecclesiology has made some significant contributions to ecumenical discussions, reading the impact of eucharistic ecclesiology on the internal life of the Orthodox churches is more difficult. From the Orthodox responses to *BEM*, for example, one could easily conclude that official church agencies are still much more influenced by textbook scholasticism than by the works of Afanasiev or Zizioulas. Blame for this should not be laid solely on ponderous officialdom. Modern Orthodox (or for that matter Catholic or Protestant) appropriations of Ignatius have certain inherent limitations which make their application to modern church life problematic.

Exponents of eucharistic ecclesiology have tended to uphold an idealized second-century church order as normative in every detail for all ages and situations, and they have been inclined to ignore or dismiss evidence not conforming to that model. They have not taken seriously enough either the ecclesiological diversity one finds in the New Testament texts or the many developments since the days of Ignatius. For example, Afanasiev altogether fails to address the fact that, since the third or fourth century, the presbyter-centred parish has been the most common locus of Christian community. Zizioulas does acknowledge this, insisting against Afanasiev that "the local church as an entity with full ecclesiological status is the *episcopal diocese* and not the parish". In his view, the emergence of the presbyter-centred parish "destroyed the image of the church as a community in which all orders are necessary as *constitutive* elements", ultimately making both deacon and bishop and even laity redundant. But by opting for the diocese as the fundamental ecclesial organism, says Zizioulas, "the Orthodox Church has unconsciously brought about a rupture in its own eucharistic ecclesiology". At this point, he laments, one can only hope that "one day the bishop will find his proper place, which is the eucharist, and the rupture in eucharistic ecclesiology caused by the problem 'parish-diocese' will be healed".

It is alarming to learn that the church suffers from a disruption in its most vital structures so serious that for most of its historical existence it has only been able to *hope* for restoration of proper wholeness. It is even more surprising to discover how simple is the remedy Zizioulas proposes: "creation of small episcopal dioceses", which "would enable bishops really to know their flocks and be known by them" and thus "automatically improve the pastoral quality of the episcopacy", which "would reduce the load of administration which the bishops have at present, thus enabling them to function primarily as presidents of the eucharist, which is their ministry *par excellence*".

Can re-creation of the Ignatian local church really advance the church's mission of redemptive integration today, when the context in which the church is placed has changed so dramatically? In the context of the ancient *polis*, the eucharistic structures of the local church could and did powerfully proclaim and manifest Christ's victory over the divisions of this fallen world. But simply replicating those structures in today's "global village" might well perpetuate and exacerbate these divisions, by identifying the church with the special interests of this or that natural, purely human community. Without a significant infusion of "Irenaean" and "Cyprianic" elements, replication of "Ignatian" structures would inevitably lead to an absence of common witness and action on broader levels (the world, the nation, the region, even the city – for surely a megalopolis like Mexico City or Athens would have to be broken up into "smaller dioceses"). At the very least, it would result in wasteful duplication of programmes.

How has "recent" Orthodox-Catholic dialogue responded to the challenge of integrating the perspectives of Ignatius, Irenaeus and Cyprian? It is hardly surprising that eucharistic ecclesiology, especially as articulated by Zizioulas, plays a prominent role, particularly in the work of the Joint International Commission. But before examining the relevant texts in greater detail, it is important to note the broader theological context into which these texts situate their discussion of ministry and episcopacy.

Both the 1982 Munich Statement and the 1988 Valamo Statement, echoing points made elsewhere by Zizioulas, draw attention to the importance of a pneumatologically conditioned Christology for a proper understanding of ecclesiology and therefore of episcopal ministry. In contrast to "Christomonistic" approaches which see the church chiefly in terms of the structures instituted by Christ long ago, the statements call attention to the Spirit's role in constituting the church in each new moment and situation. As the anointed one of God, Christ is not an isolated individual who lived in a past which is increasingly distant from us. He "is present through the Spirit, in the church, his body, from which he cannot be separated" (Valamo, sec. 9, *The Quest for Unity*, p.132). Because Christ's ministry is present to us only through the Spirit, ecclesial ministry is necessarily *charismatic*. For the same reason, it is *relational*. The nexus of relationships established by the Spirit creates a new way of being, which transforms both the one ordained and those for whom he is ordained, making it futile to debate whether ordained ministry in the church is functional or ontological in nature. As Zizioulas writes, "In the light of love and in the context of the notion of communion, ordination binds the ordained person so deeply and existentially with the community that in his new state after ordination he cannot be conceived in himself at all – he has become a relational entity."[18] Finally, ecclesial ministry has an *eschatological* dimension. By the power of the Spirit it builds up the church so as to reveal in it the space and time of this world as "the anticipated manifestation of the final realities, the foretaste of God's kingdom" (Valamo, sec. 22, *The Quest for Unity*, p.135).

A proper understanding of the relationship of pneumatology to Christology can help to correct distortions possible in the Ignatian, Irenaean and Cyprianic approaches to *episkopé*.

– Without a pneumatological perspective, the "episcopo-centrism" of Ignatius can too easily become "episcopo-monism", in which the diverse other gifts of the Spirit in the local church are suppressed, supplanted or simply ignored, so that the bishop comes to be seen as the unique possessor and source of all spiritual gifts, rather than the one who discerns their presence and authorizes their use for the upbuilding of the community.

– Without a pneumatological perspective, the Irenaean apostolic succession can too easily be reduced to the historical transmission of authority through hands on heads, ignoring the importance of ecclesial context or even the apostolic faith itself. Similarly, the Irenaean insistence on apostolic faith can too easily be reduced to the maintenance and mechanical transmission of the faith, as though it were an inert deposit rather than a living confession.

– Without a pneumatological perspective, the Cyprianic emphasis on the unity of the episcopate can too easily detach the episcopate from the whole body of the faithful, placing it over and above the church rather than in its midst, and can degenerate into an insistence on institutional uniformity, to the detriment of true conciliarity.

I consider the great merit of Orthodox-Catholic dialogue to be this recognition of the importance of pneumatology for ecclesiology. Among other things, it has made possible a balanced and coherent understanding of the relationship of the one and the many (Ignatius), the local and the universal (Cyprian), the historical and the eschatological (Irenaeus). One of the fruits of this approach is the 1982 Munich Statement, especially Sections II and III (*The Quest for Unity*, pp.57-64), a text which merits repeated reading.

The church, the Munich Statement argues, cannot be understood simply in sociological categories. It is above all a sacramental reality which "finds its model, its origin and its purpose in the mystery of God, one in three Persons" (II.1, *The Quest for Unity*, p.58). At the same time, the church is not an abstraction. Rather, it is a "local" reality, "placed" in the midst of the world to be the prototype of renewed human community. It is a *koinonia* which most fully realizes itself in the eucharistic assembly of the local church, gathered around the bishop or the priest in communion with him as one body. This *koinonia* is eschatological, in that it anticipates the newness of the last times through continuing repentance and confession, conversion and reconciliation. It is also kerygmatic, "not only because the celebration 'announces' the event of the mystery but also because it actually realizes it today in the Spirit" (II.2, *The Quest for Unity*, p.58). Of this *koinonia*, "the entire assembly, each one according to his rank, is *leitourgos*". While being the gift of the triune God, *koinonia* is also the response of men and women who, "in the faith which comes from the Spirit and the Word... put into practice the vocation and the mission received in baptism: to become living members, in one's proper rank, of the body of Christ" (II.2, *The Quest for Unity*, p.59).

Within this context of communion, the bishop exercises a ministry which is "not merely a tactical or pragmatic function (because a president is necessary) but an organic function" which is "closely bound to the eucharistic assembly over which he presides" (II.3, *The Quest for Unity*, p.59). Within the communion of the local church, the bishop "delivers the word of salvation and the eucharistic gifts", but he also "'receives' from his church, which is faithful to tradition, the word he transmits". The bishop also "stands at the heart of the local church as minister of the Spirit to discern the charisms and take care that they are exercised in harmony, for the good of all, in faithfulness to the apostolic tradition. He puts himself at the service of the initiatives of the Spirit so that nothing may prevent them from contributing to building up *koinonia*."

After thus developing the Ignatian aspect of the bishop's ministry, the Munich Statement considers the Irenaean question of apostolic succession. The communion of the bishop and his community "lies within the communion of the apostolic community" (II.4, *The Quest for Unity,* p.60).

In the ancient tradition... the bishop elected by the people – who guarantee his apostolic faith, in conformity with what the local church confesses – receives the ministerial grace of Christ by the Spirit in the prayer of the assembly and by the laying on of hands (*cheirotonia*) of the neighbouring bishops, witnesses of the faith of their own churches. His charism, coming directly from the Spirit of God, is given him in the apostolicity of his church (linked to the faith of the apostolic community) and in that of the other churches represented by their bishops.

Thus apostolic succession means more than a mere transmission of powers. "It is a succession in a church which witnesses to the apostolic faith, in communion with the other churches which witness to the same apostolic faith."

The Munich Statement then turns to the relationship between the eucharistic celebration of the local church and the communion of all the local churches as the one body of Christ (cf. Cyprian). The ontological identity of the local churches "comes from the fact that all by eating the same bread and sharing in the same cup become the same unique body of Christ into which they have been integrated by the same baptism" (III.1, *The Quest for Unity,* p.61). From this understanding that the church is a communion of local churches flows the understanding of how the bishops of the churches are related in their common responsibility for *episkopé* in the church. "Attachment to the apostolic communion binds all the bishops together, linking the *episkopé* of the local churches to the college of the apostles" (III.4, *The Quest for Unity,* p.63). "Because the one and only church is made present in his local church, each bishop cannot separate the care for his own church from that of the universal church. When, by the sacrament of ordination, he receives the charism of the Spirit for the *episkopé* of one local church, his own, by that very fact he receives the charism of the Holy Spirit for the *episkopé* of the entire church." Thus, "the *episkopé* for the universal church is seen to be entrusted, by the Spirit, to the totality of local bishops in communion with one another".

This selection of quotations from the Munich Statement suggests its theological richness. It challenges not only Orthodox and Catholics but also others engaged in the ecumenical enterprise to go beyond familiar institutional and juridical conceptions, beyond a "Christomonistic" approach to ecclesiology. At the same time, the careful reader may well ask how closely the situation described in the text actually corresponds to the life of either the Orthodox or the Catholic Church. For example, while "in the ancient tradition" the bishop may have been "elected by the people – who guarantee his apostolic faith, in conformity with what the local church confesses", is this in fact the case today?

Similarly, one may ask whether the pneumatological perspective professed by the Joint International Commission has fully penetrated all aspects of its work. An extended example from its Valamo Statement may illustrate this point.

After discussing "Christ and the Holy Spirit" (section I) and "The Priesthood in the Divine Economy of Salvation" (section II), the statement goes on to "The Ministry of the Bishop, Presbyter and Deacon" (section III). The statement emphasizes that these are not to be viewed in isolation, since "the various ministries converge in the eucharistic synaxis" (para. 24, *The Quest for Unity,* p.135). But notwithstanding the subtitle of this section of the statement, presbyters and deacons are treated only very briefly (in paras 41-43, *The Quest for Unity,* pp.138f.). Reference is made to other charisms in the church only once, when the importance of the "particular charisms" of women "for the building up of the body of Christ" is mentioned (para. 32, *The Quest for Unity,* p.137) – and the point of that paragraph is to indicate that "our churches remain faithful to the historical and theological tradition according to which they ordain only men to the priestly ministry".

The Valamo Statement is certainly "episcopo-centric", though it would be ungracious to call it "episcopo-monistic". The problem is that it fails to situate episcopacy within a broader and more comprehensive understanding of ministry. Symptomatic of this failure is its inconsistent use of the term minister/ministry. As the US Orthodox-Catholic Consultation points out in its critique of the Valamo Statement, at some points "all the baptized faithful are seen as exercising diverse ministries. At other points a distinction is implied between this general ministry of all the faithful and that of the ordained... In other cases, ministry/minister can mean only the ordained; and in at least one instance... it can mean only the one who assembles the community and presides in the celebration of the sacraments" (para. 9, *The Quest for Unity,* p.145).[19] By relying so heavily on eucharistic ecclesiology, with its essentially cultic view of ministry, the Valamo Statement missed an opportunity to develop more fully the pneumatological perspective which it sketches in its opening paragraphs.

Let us now turn from the Joint International Commission's appropriation of Ignatius to its appropriation of Irenaeus, to its understanding of apostolic succession and episcopal ordination. In the Valamo Statement, as in the earlier Munich Statement, the Commission affirms that "the apostolic tradition concerns the community and not only an isolated individual, ordained bishop" (para. 45, *The Quest for Unity,* p.139). But sometimes the Valamo Statement appears to revert to a less-nuanced conception, or at least to a now-dated vocabulary. For example, we are told that "through his ordination each bishop becomes successor of the apostles" (para. 49, *The Quest for Unity,* p.140; cf. para. 40, *The Quest for Unity,* p.138). Equally infelicitous is a sentence not yet quoted from the Munich Statement: "The bishop receives the gift of episcopal grace (1 Tim. 4:14) in the sacrament of consecration effected by bishops who themselves have received this gift, thanks to the existence of an uninterrupted series of episcopal ordinations, beginning from the holy apostles" (para. 3, *The Quest for Unity,* p.59). This appears to revert to a hands-on-heads understanding of apostolic succession. Also striking is the concluding sentence of the Valamo Statement's discussion of episcopal ordination: "What is fundamental for the incorporation of the newly elected person in the episcopal communion is that it is accomplished by the glorified Lord in the power of the Holy Spirit at the moment of the imposition of hands" (para. 27, *The Quest for Unity,* p.136). Up to this point, the text had been following practically verbatim the 1977 "Orthodox-Roman Catholic Reflections on Ministry". Why was this sentence interpolated at this point? Should it be regarded as inconsequential, or does it represent the "bottom line" of the Joint International Commission's thinking on "valid orders"?

This question has considerable ecumenical importance, since its implications go beyond the Orthodox-Catholic dialogue to their dialogue with Christian traditions lacking "apostolic succession" as it has been experienced in those two churches. On the one hand, the US Orthodox-Catholic consultation stated in its own 1986 study of "Apostolicity as God's Gift in the Life of the Church" that "apostolicity seems to consist more in fidelity to the apostles' proclamation and mission than in any one form of handing on community office" (para. 10, *The Quest for Unity*, p.128; cf. the US critique of the Valamo Statement; para. 25, *The Quest for Unity*, p.149). This statement would appear to leave room for further discussion of how the community office can be handed on without compromising apostolicity. The Joint International Commission on the other hand, seems more inclined to pit the Orthodox-Catholic understanding and experience of apostolic succession against that of other traditions. Consider these two passages from the Joint Commission's 1993 Balamand Statement on "uniatism":

> On each side it is recognized that what Christ has entrusted to his church – profession of apostolic faith, participation in the sacraments, above all the one priesthood celebrating the one sacrifice of Christ, the apostolic succession of bishops – cannot be considered the exclusive possession of one of our churches (para. 13, *The Quest for Unity*, p.177).
>
> Everyone should be informed of the apostolic succession of the other church and the authenticity of its sacramental life (para. 30, *The Quest for Unity*, p.181).

While these passages were written as part of an effort to resolve an exceptional crisis in Orthodox-Catholic relations and while the statement in which they occur was not part of the Commission's original agenda, they do suggest that Catholics and Orthodox may have difficulty maintaining their professed pneumatological perspective on ecclesiology when they leave the rarefied realm of pure theological discussion for the real world of interchurch relations.

While the work of the US Orthodox-Catholic Theological Consultation has been less voluminous than that of the Joint International Commission and has not directly addressed the subject of episcopacy, it may have implications for the broader issues raised in this paper.

At many points the statements of the US Consultation reveal the same Ignatian perspective as we have seen in those of the Joint International Commission. Sometimes however they sound a more Irenaean note, especially in the 1986 agreed statement on "Apostolicity as God's Gift in the Life of the Church". It affirms that "we call the church apostolic first of all because the church continues to share this mission [namely, that of the apostles, who were 'endowed with the authority and freedom to act authentically on behalf of the one who sent them'] in history, continues to be authorized by the risen Lord, through its continuing structures, as his legitimate representative" (para. 5, *The Quest for Unity*, p.126). But in addition to this historical aspect, apostolicity has an eschatological dimension, so that "here and now the life of the church – whether expressed in authoritative teaching, in judgment and discipline or in the eucharist itself – is being molded, corrected and governed by what has been received from the past *and* by what is awaited at the last day" (para. 7, *The Quest for Unity*, pp.126f.). So also, when we speak of our faith as apostolic, we do not mean simply that its content has been received from the apostles. The *depositum fidei* is not "an inert object, relayed in purely mechanical fashion from generation to generation by duly authorized ministers" (para. 8, *The Quest for Unity*, p.127). Rather, it remains a living confession, both content and act. In the life of the church and of each Christian, apostolicity is continually experienced in the baptismal act of receiving and giving back the church's apostolic faith. "Apostolicity therefore is by no means unique to or limited to the realm of hierarchical ministry. For just as we share by baptism in the royal and prophetic priesthood, so also by this baptismal confession we too become bearers of the church's apostolicity" (para. 9, *The Quest for Unity*, p.127).

Within this broader context, what can be said of "those structures which attest to and assure the unity of the churches in their apostolic confession" (para. 11, *The Quest for Unity*, p.128)? The US Consultation returned to this question in its 1989 agreed statement on "Conciliarity and Primacy in the Church". The church, both locally and universally, is the locus of ordered charisms. Within the local eucharistic community "permanent offices of leadership have been established... as a service of love and a safeguard of unity in faith and life" (para. 5, *The Quest for Unity*, p.153); but the same Spirit who sets in order the local church also "manifests his presence in the institutions which keep local communities in an ordered and loving communion with one another". The text goes on to add that "the two institutions, mutually dependent and mutually limiting, which have exercised the strongest influence on maintaining the ordered communion of the churches since apostolic times, have been the gathering of bishops and other appointed local leaders in synods, and the primacy or recognized pre-eminence of one bishop among his episcopal colleagues" (para. 6, *The Quest for Unity*, pp.153f.). Holding together these two important aspects of the Cyprianic conception of episcopal ministry remains the greatest problem still to be resolved by the Orthodox-Catholic dialogue.

As this perusal of documents resulting from international and US Orthodox-Catholic dialogue suggests, the two churches for the most part share a common understanding and practice of ministry, including episcopal ministry. The chief point in dispute is "the particular form of primacy among the churches exercised by the bishops of Rome" ("Conciliarity and Primacy", para. 7, *The Quest for Unity*, p.154). Their agreement is evident in the common affirmations set forth in those documents, as well as in the critical observations by the US Consultation on the ministry section of *BEM*:

> In general, the document *BEM* presents as possible, even laudable opinions, certain aspects of ordained ministry that we consider normative for the church's life and structure. These normative aspects include the threefold ministry; the historical succession of office holders in the episcopal ministry; the exclusive conferral of ordination by those entrusted with the *episkopé* of the community; and the presidency of the eucharist exclusively by an ordained minister...
>
> In addition to the document's emphasis on *episkopé* as necessary ministry in the church, we affirm that episcopal office is a constitutive element of the structure of the church (*Quest for Unity*, p.74).

The fact that Catholics and Orthodox can make such statements together suggests that wider reconciliation, encompassing those groups which do not regard such aspects of ministry as normative, may indeed be difficult to achieve. Nevertheless, the wealth of theological reflection on ministry offered in the principal documents of Orthodox-Catholic dialogue may provide some new perspectives for all who are engaged in the quest for Christian unity and may enrich future discussion of this central ecumenical issue.

NOTES

1 Most conveniently available in English, with further bibliographical orientation, in John Borelli and John H. Erickson, eds, *The Quest for Unity: Orthodox and Catholics in Dialogue*, Crestwood NY, St Vladimir's Seminary Press, and Washington DC, United States Catholic Conference, 1996, pp.131-42 and 53-64 respectively.

2 *Ibid,.* pp.152-55 and 65-88 respectively.

3 *Ibid.*, pp.120-24, 125-30 and 152-55 respectively.

4 "Reflexions de théologiens Orthodoxes et Catholiques sur les ministères", *La Documentation Catholique*, no. 1738, 9 March 1978, pp.262-65 (Engl. tr. in *Origins*, pp.702-704). Catholic participants in these discussions included Charles Moeller, Pierre Duprey, Louis Bouyer, Gustave Martelet and Jean-Marie Tillard; Orthodox included Metropolitan Damaskinos of Tranoupolis (now of Switzerland), Ion Bria, John Zizioulas and, in the earlier meetings, Bishop Vassilios of Aristis and Olivier Clément. These discussions appear to have been undertaken in order to "jump-start" official international Orthodox-Catholic dialogue.

5 These include "La continuité aves les origines apostoliques dans la conscience théologique des Eglises orthodoxes", *Istina*, Vol. 19, 1974, pp.65-94 (Eng. tr. "Apostolic Continuity and Orthodox Theology: Towards a Synthesis of Two Perspectives", *St Vladimir's Theological Quarterly*, Vol. 19, 1975, pp.75-108; repr. in *Being as Communion*, Crestwood, NY, St Vladimir's Seminary Press, 1985, pp.171-208); "Episkopé and Episkopos in the Early Church: A Brief Survey of the Evidence", in *Episkopé and Episcopate in Ecumenical Perspective*, Geneva, WCC, 1979; "Episkopé et Episkopos dans l'Eglise primitive", *Irénikon*, Vol. 56, 1983, pp.484-501; "The Bishop in the Theological Doctrine of the Orthodox Church", *Kanon*, Vol. 7, Vienna, 1985, pp.23-38.

6 "The Bishop in the Theological Doctrine of the Orthodox Church", p.26.

7 Cf. Kallistos Ware, "Patterns of Episcopacy in the Early Church and Today: An Orthodox View", in Peter Moore, ed., *Bishops, But What Kind? Reflections on Episcopacy*, London, SPCK, 1982, pp.1-2.

8 *Ibid.*, p.2.

9 Zizioulas, "The Bishop in the Theological Doctrine of the Orthodox Church", p.35.

10 Ware, *loc. cit.*, p.12.

11 Zizioulas, *loc. cit.*, p.35.

12 *Ibid.*

13 On this subject see my paper "The Code of Canons of the Oriental Churches (1990): A Development Favoring Relations between the Churches?", Salamanca, 1996; forthcoming in *The Jurist* and elsewhere in translation.

14 "Roman Catholic and Orthodox Dialogue: The Larger Picture", *Ecumenism*, Vol. 107, 1992, p.31.

15 Letter to the Russian princes, in Miklosich and Mueller, *Acta et diplomata*, Vienna, 1860, p.521. On "Eastern papism", see A. Pavlov, "Teoriia vostochnogo papisma v novieshei russkoi literature kanonicheskogo prava", *Pravoslavnoe Obozreniie*, 1879.

16 In "Episkopé and Episkopos in the Early Church", *loc. cit.*

17 "The Local Church in a Perspective of Communion", in *Being as Communion*, p.133; cf. his more fully articulated statement of the same point in "Apostolic Continuity and Orthodox Theology", *loc. cit.*

18 "Ordination and Communion", *Study Encounter*, Vol. 6, no. 4, p.190.

[19] Cf. also the US Consultation's comments about the earlier Munich Statement: "The text should have discussed the diversity of ministries within the one body (cf. II.1, para. 4); likewise, some reference to the priesthood proper of all the faithful would have been in order. The relation between the bishop's ministerial priesthood and that of all the faithful is not adequately explored. The relation of the bishop and the presbyter is not sufficiently addressed" (para. 10, *The Quest for Unity*, pp.67f.).

3. THE POST-DENOMINATIONALISM OF THE CHINESE CHURCH

Gao Ying

The "post-denominationalism" which characterizes the church in China derives from two main factors: (1) the ecumenical ideal among the Protestants of China in the early 20th century; (2) the emphasis on national unity in the early 1950s in Chinese society in general.

Historical factors

Denominational history in China was short, beginning after the Opium War in 1840. Consequently, denominational loyalty was weak, and Chinese Christians found it relatively easy to give up denominationalism. For instance, among Chinese Protestants no question ever arose regarding the validity of the ministry of any particular denomination. Very few Christians, even among the clergy, had ever heard about apostolic succession or historic episcopacy. This made it easier for Christians in China to begin to emphasize the need for interdenominational cooperation and church unity.

The theological point of departure was Jesus' prayer for his disciples recorded in John 17:20-21. This text shaped ecumenical thinking among Chinese Protestants for much of the 20th century. Already in 1907 the declaration on church unity from the Centenary Conference in Shanghai questioned the proliferation of separate Christian communities as something which detracted from the missionary witness of the church and undermined visible Christian unity in a non-Christian country such as China. That the desire for unity was taking shape among the Christians in China is substantiated by the testimonies of a number of missionaries, including Bishop Logan Roots, who linked the question of Christian mission to that of patriotism:

> The leading Christians of China undoubtedly believe that one reason why they should be Christians and propagate Christianity in China is that they will therefore render the

greatest service to their country; and therefore Christian zeal has become to many a matter of patriotic obligation.[1]

The idea of Christian unity was thus very much on the minds of the Chinese delegates who gathered in Edinburgh three years later to attend the first World Missionary Conference. Dr Cheng Jing-yi, already one of the outstanding ecumenical leaders of his generation, addressed the question of unity as something which should be seen as essential in the Christian federation movement in order to strengthen the church in the service of the Chinese nation and more effectively to propagate the Christian gospel. He spoke from the floor about the importance of Christian unity in his famous seven-minute speech:

> Since the Chinese Christians have enjoyed the sweetness of such a unity, we long for more, and look forward for yet greater things. Speaking plainly, we hope to see, in the near future, a united Christian church without any denominational distinctions. This may seem somewhat peculiar to some of you, but, friends, do not forget to view us from our standpoint, and if you fail to do that, the Chinese will remain always as a mysterious people to you![2]

Both Roots and Cheng recognized that Christian unity was important in China for practical as well as theological reasons, but that this unity was not one founded on Western terms. Neither the Western powers nor the denominational structures could determine the pattern of national or Christian unity in China, as developments over the next forty years would clearly indicate. The increasing ecumenical activity during those decades did bear fruit. In this regard, the formation of the Holy Catholic Church of China (Anglican), the National Christian Council and the Church of Christ in China were significant.[3]

The Protestant missionary movement of the 19th century paved the way for the ecumenical movement which came to fruition in the 20th century.[4]

Social impact

Ecumenical unity as such was never articulated as a goal of the Three-Self Patriotic Movement, the Christian mass movement launched in the early 1950s in search of Chinese Christians' selfhood and independence. No meeting was held to discuss doctrinal differences or to promote organic union. Yet there was increasing practical cooperation among Christians working together, due to the concrete needs of the situation.[5]

After the formation of the People's Republic of China in 1949, a fervent desire emerged among the people all over the country for national unity, especially since China had been so divided by both Western colonial powers and civil lords, and the people had suffered under "semi-colonial" and "semi-feudalistic" rule. The idea of national unity became the slogan everywhere. The call "With one heart and concerted efforts, build up a new united China" was heard throughout China in those days.

Because national unity was not only emphasized by the government but was also very much in the people's minds, questions arose among Protestant Christians as to why similar Christian groups were not united. Under these circumstances, the church groups found it difficult to justify their separateness before the world. The disunity of the churches also posed serious practical problems for the Protestant churches. Such divisions weakened the Christian community before the eyes of those outside and made it difficult for the government to relate to Chinese Protestants as a group that shared common concerns. This was reinforced by the foreign identity of Chinese churches, whose divisions seemed to recall the competition among the various powers in "semi-colonial" China. It was from this point of view that unity was interpreted in terms of "Love-Country-Love-Church".[6]

Chinese Protestants thus came to criticize their own disunity theologically, arguing that an unwillingness to practise tolerance and forgiveness was an expression of narrow self-centredness and arrogant individualism.

In the meantime some form of cooperation between denominations was becoming absolutely necessary. As Bishop K.H. Ting pointed out, "The most important thing at present is not unity but whole-hearted cooperation and close relations plus mutual love. Everyone must first put aside their prejudices so that we may have something of mutual tolerance."[7] The assumption was that Protestants could not come together all at once, but they could at least practice tolerance, forgiveness and mutual respect in relating to one another. The most distinctive feature of the unity at that time was based on the principle of "mutual respect in matters of faith". On one level mutual respect could be understood as the ecumenical counterpart of "seeking the common ground while reserving differences".[8]

The practical concerns facing the institutional churches and the long-standing desire for a united Protestantism interacted, and Chinese Protestants became increasingly unified in the 1950s. Although separate denominational structures would be maintained at least through 1958, the necessity of Christian cooperation made them increasingly insignificant in the life of the Protestant community.[9]

Given the short history of denominationalism, which diminished Christians' denominational loyalty even before 1949, together with the impact of Chinese society on the church after 1949, the feeling of disinterestedness in denominational identity grew among Chinese Christians. Chinese Protestant leaders had been saying for years that there was no justification for denominationalism in China, that denominations were "imports" and in no way intrinsic to Christian witness. So when the end finally came, it should not have come as a surprise to anyone.[10]

On the whole, it was mostly non-theological and non-ecclesiastical factors which contributed to the entry of the Chinese church onto the post-denominational stage. Forty years later, the key principle to which Chinese Christians now adhere in remaining post-denominational is still that of "mutual respect in matters of faith and worship". This principle ensures that denominational particularities are not obliterated but respected and maintained. The pattern is that of "unity without uniformity". Under this principle, services of congregational worship are held both on Sundays and Sabbath days, baptism is by immersion as well as by sprinkling in several historical traditions to suit the habits and likings of different Christians.

In the realm of church order, besides the two traditional Anglican bishops K.H. Ting and Stephen Shen-yin Wang, two ecumenical bishops were consecrated in 1988. They did not play an administrative role as diocesan bishops. As Bishop Ting pointed out in the sermon he preached on the occasion of their consecration, bishops have their authority, but this is based not on any written constitutional stipulation or executive position, but on their spiritual, moral, theological and pastoral ministry. The better they serve, the greater their authority and the people's readiness to listen. The more democratic they are, the more powerful are their appeals.

Unfortunately, the two newly consecrated bishops have passed away in recent years. I understand that at present some of the leaders do not see fit to ordain new bishops. In my personal opinion, the China Christian Council, which has elected a new president and chairperson of the Three Self Patriotic Movement, and whose prestige needs to be built up, should not be overshadowed by a new bishop.

Some concerns

1. Obstacles to church unity

Our unity in the China Christian Council is still "post-denominational". It is not yet the unity of a United Church of Christ of China. As noted earlier, unity does not mean uniformity in the practice of Chinese Protestantism. There are still historical and theological differences that separate Chinese Christian communities from one another, although these differences are not as sharp as they once were, nor are they reinforced by separate denominational structures. For example, Seventh-day Adventists no longer insist on being called Adventists, but they do meet for worship on Saturdays. Baptists continue with their practice of baptism by immersion, and indigenous church groups continue to worship in their own way.[11] Such diversity is a good thing.

The main obstacle to our church unity is the absence of a common understanding of the church and of the ministry. There is a small but strong group of Christians who call themselves the Little Flock, which can be found in almost all parts of China. They do not believe in ordination or in accepting any leadership by women on the ground of their interpretation of the priesthood of all believers. They disapprove of the idea of any clergy and, ecclesiologically, recognize nothing beyond the local group of the saved as "church". They are happy to stay within the China Christian Council, but they reject the idea of going one step further to form the United Church of China with an ordained ministry and nationwide organization.

Some years ago there was a proposal from certain church leaders that the Seventh-day Adventists, the Little Flock and the True Jesus Christ Church should be allowed to re-establish their denominations. We would still be post-denominational in the sense that Presbyterians, Lutherans, Methodists, Episcopalians and so on would be post-denominational. In other words, there would be four denominations in China, one large and three small. But most of the church leaders considered that this would be a step backwards, and the proposal was not accepted.

Thus, post-denominational unity is as far as we can go at present. The non-theological and non-ecclesiastical factors obliged us to move too quickly into the post-denominational stage – hence we are left with many unsolved problems. Although we are aware of the fragility of our unity, we do not want to do things that injure, and we wait for the guidance of the Holy Spirit to show us the next step forward.

2. Implementation of "mutual respect"

One has to recognize that different theological, liturgical and devotional inclinations continued to exist among Christians even when denominationalism was abandoned. Hence the need for mutual respect. However, mutual respect in matters of faith and worship is sometimes easier said than done. Those in the majority and those holding positions of power may easily refuse to see the point of respecting minority characteristics and particularities. Mutual respect is a principle that calls for deep Christian love in its implementation.

The opening up of China to the outside world has tested the strength of our post-denominational unity. The return of more institutionalized forms of church life has also meant a renewed interest in denominations among some Christians. So far there is no sign on the part of those of any denominational background to restore their denominations. Seventh-day Adventists abroad did try to restore Seventh-day Adventism in China, and a few years ago they went as far as the formation of a China Council, located in Hong Kong. But this venture came to nothing when it was opposed by former Seventh-day Adventist leaders in China.

As far as we can see in the Chinese church, those who do not feel quite at home in our post-denominational existence are mostly from three groups – the Little Flock, the Seventh-day Adventists and members of the former True Jesus Church. A lack of due attention to their particular characteristics produced in them in a tendency to exaggerate certain special points in the content of their faith to the neglect of our commonality in the basic faith in Jesus Christ as Lord and Saviour.

3. Theoretical formation of unity

Historically, the Chinese are known for their spirit of tolerance. In the third century B.C.E., for example, Mencius maintained that human nature is good while Xun-zi maintained that human nature is evil. Later thinkers sought to mediate these two opposite positions. All these different positions were acceptable among the classic Confucian scholars. There was no attempt to rule which one was to be the orthodoxy, with the others being heresies. Among Chinese Buddhists, different interpretations of Buddhist faith were also permissible. There has been no seat of ultimate authority on matters of faith in Chinese Confucianism, Taoism or Buddhism. The question was not even raised in the intellectual history of China.

This intellectual legacy is in the blood of Chinese Christians as well. Inheriting this spirit of tolerance, the China Christian Council embodies a very wide range of unity, ecclesiologically and theologically. We are thankful to God for that unity which includes for all practical purposes all Protestants in the country, but we are also aware that human weakness and pride may sometimes result in a lack of creativity for the sake of maintaining the unity itself. A theological articulation of Christian unity was not desirable in the beginning, because any theological controversy would have been divisive.

Unlike efforts towards Christian unity in other parts of the world, Christian unity in China was not achieved through a lengthy process of theological discussion and planning. Beginning in 1951, it took place almost all at once, both as a result of the common Christian confession of "one Lord, one faith, one baptism" and of the practical and concrete needs of the churches.

The Christian church in China has been unusually blessed by the guidance of the Holy Spirit in the past five decades. This experience will in time find expression theologically to the enrichment of truly trinitarian Christian faith. The church will also need to interpret its unity more clearly. The point is not to argue for a rigidly defined confessional orthodoxy that would go against the grain of Chinese Christian experience up to this point, but to articulate a theological and ecclesiological centre for Christian unity in China.[12] But we have learned from the history of the Christian church and from our early Western missionary colleagues not to attempt to do too many things in too short a time.

4. Formation for ecumenical sharing

The China Christian Council is different from a national council of denominational churches because Chinese Protestantism is post-denominational. While it aims to be a service agency to all Protestant Christian groups in China, its ecclesial nature has grown, as shown by the publication in 1992 of its generally accepted Faith and Order document. Thus it was quite correct for it to be admitted to the World Council of Churches as a full member church and not as an associate (national) council of churches. At the same time, the China Christian Council has been watching discussions in Faith and Order over the past years. We believe that it is a pity that the developments in China seem not yet to have been regarded as a phenomenon worthy of serious study. When friends talk with us personally, they usually have a lot of good things to say about our post-denominationalism, but we do not know how many of them are taking it seriously.

Christians in China do think that the step which the church in China has taken is an important one for world Christianity. Of course, nothing is perfectly right from its beginning. We like to think that ours is an experiment on behalf of the worldwide church.[13]

Therefore, it is appreciated that the WCC now pays attention to the Chinese experiment, offering this opportunity to share with you at this Faith and Order consultation. It is my hope that this sharing will not only help other churches to understand better the post-denominationalism of the Chinese church, but also to help us by channeling experiences of other churches to us.

NOTES

[1] World Missionary Conference, *Co-operation and the Promotion of Unity,* Edinburgh, Oliphant, Anderson and Ferrier, 1910, Vol. 8, p.83.

[2] *Ibid.,* p.85.

[3] Cf. Philip L. Wickeri, *Seeking the Common Ground,* Maryknoll NY, Orbis, 1988, pp.217-25.

[4] *Ibid.,* pp. 216-25.

[5] *Ibid.,* pp. 223-42.

[6] *Ibid.,* pp. 215-26.

[7] "On the Unity of the Church", *TF,* no. 218, 17 June 1950, p.271.

[8] Wickeri, *op. cit.,* pp.215-30.

[9] *Ibid.,* pp.216-27.

[10] *Ibid.,* pp.216-27.

[11] *Ibid.,* pp.233-42.

[12] *Ibid.,* pp.233-42.

[13] Church Unity and Ecumenicity", an interview with Bishop K.H. Ting by Claudia and Gotthard Oblau, 1991.

4. *EPISKOPÉ* AND EPISCOPACY IN SOME RECENT BILATERAL DIALOGUES

Stephen Sykes

The Church of England (with the episcopal churches of Ireland, Wales and Scotland) has recently established a communion of churches with the Lutheran churches of Finland, Iceland, Norway, Sweden, Estonia and Latvia on the basis of the Porvoo Common Statement and Declaration (1993). The earlier (1991) Meissen Declaration between the Church of England and the German Evangelical Churches, which explicitly agreed "to establish forms of joint oversight" (*"Formen gemeinsamer geistlicher Aufsicht zu schaffen"*)(B2), did not so fully bring into being "a reconciled, common ministry" (*"ein gemeinsames, in vollem Einklang befindliches Amt"*) (B7). A further theological conference on *episkopé* and episcopacy between the Meissen partners has taken place, and seemed (to one participant at least) to make important progress. Meanwhile, the Leuenberg Church Fellowship invited Anglicans into their conversations, conscious that these developments impinged on its common life. And the Episcopal Church in the USA, independently but not without wider consultation, has produced with the Evangelical Lutheran Church in America "The Implications of the Gospel" (1988), "Towards Full Communion" and "Concordat of Agreement". These developments, which have yet to be agreed by representative church bodies, specifically involve the transcending of old disagreements about *episkopé* and episcopacy.

These developments are well-known. Here I shall offer some reflections on why they were possible and on their significance for the future of the ecumenical movement. In my view these developments represent no small achievement. The issues are not minor ones, nor are the agreements uncontroversial – as is shown by the fact that it has not so far proved possible for the Church of Denmark and the Evangelical-Lutheran Church of Latvia to participate in the Porvoo Communion. The outcome of the Concordat has yet to be determined. But I can personally testify to the change of relationship which has come about as a result of these developments in Northern Europe and North America, and the outcomes can be offered to other churches in fellowship and prayer for their discernment and reception.

Reasons for success

There are three principal reasons for the success of these developments:

1. *The relatively light incidence of authoritative, traditional material on* episkopé *and episcopacy and the absence of any official condemnations.*

In this area, Anglicans and Lutherans have made the furthest advances, Anglicans and United churches the next best, and Anglican and Reformed churches the least progress. This is entirely what one would expect, given the histories of the various churches since the European Reformation. But as a group these churches are all characterized by relatively uncomplicated traditions. The principal Anglican sources for the doctrine of *episkopé* and episcopacy are the scripture and the ordinal(s). Neither articles nor canon law contain more than occasional hints about the nature and practice of *episkopé* and episcopacy. On the Lutheran side, although the interpretation of Articles V, VI and XXVIII of the *Confessio Augustana* raise formidable questions, there is no explicitly anti-episcopal teaching. Both the Augsburg and the Reformed confessions are clear and emphatic about the abuse of power (domination) in the church, and affirm equality of (legitimate) power and function. But they do not condemn *episkopé* and episcopacy; and writings in both traditions envisage the possibility of a positive exercise of episcopal office in accordance with the gospel.

"Towards Full Communion" contains a notably thorough piece of historical writing on "The Lutheran Churches and Episcopal Ministry" (ch. 3), which is extended and deepened in "Essays on the Church and Ministry in Northern Europe" in the Porvoo Common Statement.

In other words, these developments have emerged from an historical background whose authoritative documentation does not present obstacles as formidable as those in other traditions. As an example of what is *not* said in any classic Anglican text we may take a clause applied to bishops in Roman Catholic teaching: "invested with the fullness of the sacrament of Orders" (*Lumen Gentium*, 26). It is also not a part of any historic formularies of Anglicanism to insist that episcopacy belongs to the *esse* of the church. Moreover, the official Roman Catholic response to the Final Report of ARCIC (1991) insisted that "the Roman Catholic Church recognizes in the apostolic succession both an unbroken line of episcopal ordination from Christ through the apostles down through the centuries to the bishops of today and an uninterrupted continuity in Christian doctrine from Christ to those today who teach in union with the College of Bishops and its head, the Successor of Peter". Though certain Anglicans may believe some or even all of these propositions, none of them is embedded in Anglicanism's authoritative, traditional material.

Of course, it cannot be denied that what Anglicans do profess is sometimes seen as controversial. According to the preface to the 1662 ordinal, there have been three orders of ministry "from the apostles' time". The ordinal itself makes the point that these orders are of divine appointment; and the articles affirm that the ministration of

Word and Sacrament is carried out in Christ's name and with his commission and authority (Article XXVI). In response to the papal condemnation of Anglican orders (1896) the Archbishops of Canterbury and York stated: "The intention of our fathers was to keep and continue these offices which come down from the earliest times, and 'reverently to use and esteem them'" (*Saepius Officio*, 17).

What is affirmed and defended in the ecumenical documents we are considering is, in effect, the "reverent use and estimation" of offices of great antiquity. It is never asserted that the chain of episcopal ordinations is unbroken; rather that the present (and past) ordinations to episcopal office are, in the words of the Porvoo Common Statement, in "intended continuity from the apostles themselves" (para. 50). In this way, *episkopé* and episcopacy can be fully contextualized "within" the meaning of the apostolic gospel handed on in the church as a whole. Succession in the apostolic tradition means "continuity in the permanent characteristics" of the church of the apostles (*BEM*, Ministry, para. 34). The list of "permanent" characteristics which follows is not treated in the bilateral documents as a comprehensive, unquestioned definition of the "essence" of the church, but is altered and added to in a variety of ways. The method of "portraiture" is preferred in Porvoo Common Statement ("The Scriptures offer a portrait of a church living in the light of the gospel"; para. 20), and it is acknowledged to be both incomplete and challenging. Though the modern churches are obliged to attempt to live according to this portrait, all are similarly bound to admit to defects in their own performance. Unlike the method of defining essences, which never escapes an element of arbitrariness, portraiture does not require a church first to identify the speck in its brother's eye before recognizing the massive beam in its own. It is something of a liberation to discover that the gospel does not require one to be defensive about an episcopal pedigree.

2. A high degree of agreement on scriptural hermeneutics.

Many of the positions adopted by the churches on *episkopé* and episcopacy were formulated long before the rise of historical-critical research. Subsequently, a very different picture of the life of the early Christian communities has developed, together with theoretical studies about the processes and pressures of institution-building. Many of the ways in which rival positions were legitimated by scriptural argument or reference in the 16th and 17th centuries simply look naive by the standards of contemporary hermeneutics.

The point is formulated rather robustly in the 1987 Niagara Report of the Anglican-Lutheran Consultation on Episcopé:

> Study of the life of the early Christian communities reflected in the pages of the New Testament should make it unthinkable for us to isolate ordination at the hands of someone in linear succession to the apostles as the sole criterion of faithfulness to the apostolic commission. So many investigations have now confirmed this conclusion that the burden of proof has passed to those who would argue otherwise. Ministries of pastoral leadership, co-ordination and oversight have continuously been part of the church's witness to the gospel. Indeed we may say that the mission of the church required the coherence of its witness in every aspect of its life, and that this coherence required supervision. But the New Testament does not entitle us to assert that such supervision was carried out by a uniform structure of government inherited directly from or transmitted by the apostles... Thus to speak of "apostolic succession" is to speak primarily of characteristics of the

whole church; and to recognize a church as being "in the apostolic succession" is to use not one criterion of discernment, but many (cf. *BEM*, Ministry, para. 35).

The same report went on to cite ARCIC's Final Report on Ministry and Ordination (1973):

> The New Testament shows that ministerial office played an essential part in the life of the church in the first century, and we believe that the provision of a ministry of this kind is part of God's design for his people. Normative principles governing the purpose and function of the ministry are already present in the New Testament documents (e.g. Mark 10:43-45; Acts 20:28; 1 Tim. 4:12-16; 1 Pet. 5:1-4). The early churches may well have had considerable diversity in the structure of pastoral ministry, though it is clear that some churches were headed by ministers who were called *episcopoi* and *presbyteroi*. While the first missionary churches were not a loose aggregation of autonomous communities, we have no evidence that "bishops" and "presbyters" were appointed everywhere in the primitive period. The terms "bishop" and "presbyter" could be applied to the same man or to men with identical or very similar functions. Just as the formation of the canon of the New Testament was a process incomplete until the second half of the second century, so also the full emergence of the threefold ministry of bishop, presbyter and deacon required a longer period than the apostolic age. Thereafter this threefold structure became universal in the church (para. 6).

It is therefore a serious matter when the official Roman Catholic response objects to ARCIC's interpretation of Scripture in the following terms:

> As is well known, the Catholic doctrine affirms that the historical-critical method is not sufficient for the interpretation of Scripture. Such interpretation cannot be separated from the living Tradition of the Church which receives the message of Scripture.

How is this comment to be evaluated specifically with reference to *episkopé* and episcopacy?

In the first place, it may readily be agreed on hermeneutical grounds that one should not "separate" Tradition (understood as the Holy Spirit's active keeping of the church within the truth) from critical enquiry, which is another mode of the Holy Spirit's guidance and is also specifically concerned with truth. An incarnational faith cannot be cavalier about historical fact. It would in fact amount to separation if historical fact were held to be irrelevant to matters on which the judgment of earlier centuries had been given. The proper question to ask is, what is to be included within Tradition?

Second, it may well be said that Tradition is in practice ignored if it is insisted that the relatively uncontroversial development of *episkopé* and episcopacy in the first and second centuries was a decline from more primitive standards of church government. There are those scholars who write as though the Pastoral Epistles represent a sad falling away from Pauline standards of immediacy and grace. There are also those for whom Paul himself represents an unacceptable compromise with the radicalism of Jesus' own message. Scholars are of course entitled to make such judgments, but they pass on very serious theological questions for others to consider. For example, one is bound to ask whether the church could be enjoying the guidance of the Holy Spirit at the same time as it was seriously misunderstanding the implications of the gospel, a misunderstanding which it proceeded to embody in its structures.

The question is serious and searching; but it is not necessary to deploy it about *every* development of the later centuries. It bears, rather, on *major* developments. Nor is it required that each major development should be regarded as incapable of being subject to critical scrutiny or of improvement and further development. It may be admitted, for example, that there are negative costs to be paid in relation to a generally positive outcome.

This argument bears directly upon *episkopé* and episcopacy. The development of a specific form of episcopacy cannot be regarded as supra-historical. The historicity of the development is ground for its provisionality, and opens the requirement for criticism and reformation in the light of the gospel. At the same time it gives "relative justification" to all the forms which have arisen in the course of history.[1] It is a feature of the ecumenical documents with which we are concerned that they accord a relative historical justification to episcopacy, but subordinate the institution to the requirements of the gospel. To cite the Porvoo again:

> The church is a divine reality, holy and transcending present finite reality; at the same time, as a human institution, it shares the brokenness of human community in its ambiguity and frailty. The church is always called to repentance, reform and renewal, and has constantly to depend on God's mercy and forgiveness (para. 20).

3. A common view on the relation of justification by grace and church structures.

A vital consensus on this subject has been formulated in the 1994 report of the Lutheran-Roman Catholic Joint Commission, "Church and Justification":

> Above all... it is agreed that all institutional or structural elements of church continuity are and remain instruments of the gospel, which alone creates and sustains the church, not in their own right but only insofar and as long as they testify to the continuity of the church and serve that continuity. Their effectiveness as signs and means of the continuity of the church is limited and called in question when and for as long as their relatedness to and transparency for that gospel are diminished or obscured.

The use of the terms "signs", "means" and "instruments" in this text can be correlated with the stress laid in the Niagara Report on the church as an integrated system of communication, and the section on the historic episcopate as sign in Porvoo, paras 50-54. Both these texts acknowledge what "Church and Justification" makes explicit when it says that "special care is needed to see to it that these instruments and signs of institutional continuity do not cease to function as servants of the gospel, not even when one seems obligated to grant them an ecclesially indispensable and binding character" (181).

The creativity of both Porvoo and the Concordat lies in the fact that, in different ways, judgments have been made which permit the overcoming of an historic impasse. On the Lutheran side, freedom is claimed to embrace the sign of episcopal consecration in historic succession, given unhesitating Anglican acknowledgment of the primacy of the gospel. On the Anglican side, the strict requirement of reordination has been laid aside, given Lutheran assent to the value and use of the sign of historic episcopal succession. Both sides confirm in various ways that no church-dividing obstacles exist in each other's confessional documents; and, vitally, both sides recognize that participation in each other's common life is a necessary implication of that degree of communion established by the agreements. With the Niagara Report all these documents lay heavy stress on the apostolic, missionary character of *episkopé* and episcopacy. It is not seen as a bureaucratic function.

In this connection the issue of power is exceptionally important and needs explicit treatment. Experience suggests that churches which do not have bishops (and some which do!) view bishops negatively as authoritarians and hierarchs engaged in the relentless expansion of their own powers. The matter needs to be set in a rather larger context than is normally invoked. All institutions distribute and exercise powers, and do so unequally. Some persons have more of it, some have less. In addition to the formal hierarchies there are also informal ones. Bureaucracies are said to be service organizations, but bureaucrats and their secretaries have great opportunities to influence decisions by positive and negative means. It would appear that everyone recognizes these facts; but it is remarkable how little theological attention they receive in the life of the church.

Moreover, after Michel Foucault we can no longer be naive about the power bestowed by knowledge, including theological knowledge. It is not credible to identify those who occupy the hierarchies of order as bearing powers, and ignore the powers of the theologically articulate elites. When our Lord opposes the dominative strategies of the powerful of his own day and warns his disciples against exercising power in such a way, his target is not merely a future hierarchical church structure.

Justification by grace is the entry into a life of humility. It is sacramentally expressed in baptism, and baptismal equality is the unique inheritance of every Christian. The powers which are necessarily and unavoidably exercised by many people in the church must be subject to the scrutiny of justifying grace. The bestowal or acquisition of power, whether of orders or by bureaucratic appointment, is invariably attended by temptation. Institutional expression needs to be given to the principle that Christians are mutually accountable to one another. The tendency to build walls of invulnerability around one's powers needs to be openly acknowledged, and places and times should be found where painful or critical things can be uttered in safety about how power is, or is perceived to be, exercised.

The advantage of an open episcopate is that responsibility is publicly obvious and personal; devious or manipulative behaviour is always easier in secret. Committees tend to distribute powers without personal identification. A useful way of approaching the question of *episkopé* and episcopacy in so-called non-episcopal churches might be by discovering, with sociological help, who exercises power and how. Comparisons with episcopal churches may then be developed, which may give rise to less anxiety about the supposed "authoritarianism" of "hierarchical" office-holders. Attention can also be drawn to the ways in which episcopal churches incorporate opportunities for the open discussion of how bishops discharge their responsibilities. In the Anglican case this crucially involves synods of bishops, priests and laity.

Ecumenical significance

In this paper I have attempted to identify three reasons for the success of the developments involving Anglican, Lutheran and United churches. Their significance for the future of ecumenical dialogues I consider to be great. Of course institutions endlessly reproduce the structures and ideas which validate continuing division. Though it is always difficult to overcome the historic reasons for separation, the obstacles in the Anglican-Lutheran case (as distinct from certain others) have not been so very extensive. Greater difficulties can be expected in other dialogues.

The two factors I regard as holding the greatest promise for the future are, respectively, biblical study of the ministry in the early communities (combined with an explicitly articulated theological hermeneutic), and enquiry into the theological significance of power, or rather powers, within the church.

NOTE

[1] Cf. Paul Hoffmann, "Priestertum und Amt im Neuen Testament: Eine kritische Bestandsaufnahme", in *Priesterkirche*, Düsseldorf, 1987, pp.12-61.

5. THE EXPERIENCE OF SHARED OVERSIGHT

Hugh Cross

In this paper I shall describe the background to the appointment of the first ecumenical moderator and something of the experience of the exercise of that office from 1991 to 1995, then reflect on certain questions arising from this.

The setting for the experiment of having an ecumenical moderator was Milton Keynes, a "new city" about 90 km. north of London. Since the late 1960s the city has been built partly on open space and partly by incorporating 13 small villages and several towns. The projected population by the year 2020 is 250,000. From the outset, the churches in the area agreed to work together according to the Lund principle. One consequence of this was the evolution of 23 united congregations of Anglicans and other non-Roman Catholic and non-Orthodox denominations (out of a total of 66 parishes and congregations). Because of that early decision by the churches' leadership, the growth of ecumenical understanding and trust has put Milton Keynes at the forefront of ecumenical advance, which is recognized even beyond the boundaries of the United Kingdom.

A pastoral president

The ecumenical nature and commitment of church life in Milton Keynes meant that there was continuous experiment and change. As the city grew and developed, so did the churches' mission to the city. In consequence, the church leaders, functioning collectively as the presidency of the Milton Keynes Christian Council, were increasingly expected to attend meetings and other functions in the city together, both to show their own church's commitment to the ecumenical vision and to demonstrate their approval of what was happening. Each had a much wider area of responsibility, and all found it more and more difficult to fulfill the increasing demands of the new city without doing disservice to other commitments.

The ecumenical officer, Gethin Abraham-Williams, suggested that each take a turn in serving for a two-year period as pastoral president of the Milton Keynes Christian Council. One of them would give more time to the new city while the others were freed to fulfill their normal denominational duties elsewhere. The two-year appointment had the practical advantage of a short-term assignment while demonstrating to the churches – and society in general – that one could represent all, thus serving as a measure of their unity. This scheme worked very well.

Gethin Abraham-Williams had made this suggestion in the light of research and development taking place elsewhere in England at that time, hoping that this might be a way for Milton Keynes to add its own contribution to the subject of ecumenical pastoral oversight. Two elements in this research are particularly worth mentioning.

The first was a report produced by a working party in Swindon, another developing area in the west of England. Here, out of the practical experience of personal pastoral oversight for all the churches by an Anglican assistant bishop, Bishop Freddie Temple, a report was produced in 1979 entitled, *A Bishop for All Churches in Thamesdown* (Thamesdown was the wider area, similar to the Borough of Milton Keynes). This report suggested that the ecumenical bishop should exercise personal oversight *in council*. He would share his authority with a missionary council drawn from ordained and lay representatives of the congregations and traditions in the area. The report was widely read and acclaimed, but was never implemented in Thamesdown for reasons which we need not go into here.

This "Swindon Report", as it came to be known, was one of several documents considered at a consultation on ecumenical oversight convened by the Consultative Committee for Local Ecumenical Projects in England in Windsor in the early 1980s. This consultation was part of the studies then being made in preparation for the hoped-for covenant between the Church of England, the Methodist Church, the Moravian Church and the United Reformed Church. While the covenant was not implemented, Milton Keynes did not let the work perish, but honed it to their own needs.

So, as the 1980s came to an end and the five church leader presidents had each filled a term as pastoral president of the Milton Keynes Christian Council, it was agreed to appoint a pastoral president who would live in the city and function as the ecumenical bishop of Milton Keynes.

The ecumenical moderator

Detailed planning preceded this appointment. Each denomination agreed to contribute an equal share to the budget, which meant that the person appointed would not be financially bound to any one denomination. Each church leader agreed that the ecumenical moderator would be his representative, and gave the appointee such authority as he was legally able to give. It will be recognized that this effectively meant that the ecumenical moderator would have no legal authority at all. Nevertheless, the ecumenical moderator was to hold the status of a church leader and would preside over meetings of the presidency of the Milton Keynes Christian Council.

The title "bishop" was not used because for some it would raise positive expectations of authority and jurisdiction which could not be fulfilled, while for others the term had negative resonances arising from history. While "moderator" is the title used by one of the churches for its leadership, it was not felt this would raise the wrong expectations; moreover, the title has come increasingly to be used in ecumenical circles to provide inclusive language for an office of responsibility.

According to the carefully worked-out job description, the ecumenical moderator was to:

– exercise visionary and pastoral leadership;
– be a local focus of unity;
– visit, encourage and stir up the churches ecumenically;
– challenge the denominational structures;
– develop new styles of ecumenical leadership in relation to local and regional denominational leaders.

The practice of ecumenical oversight

When I was appointed the first ecumenical moderator of Milton Keynes at the beginning of 1991, it was clear to me that the primary task of the ecumenical moderator was one of pastoral care for the servants of the churches, both ordained and lay, as well as the congregations and people of the parishes covered. The ecumenical moderator would properly fulfill the personal and collegial functions of the bishop as chief pastor for the diocese, sharing pastoral care with clergy and ministers.

This aspect of the job was of special importance to me for two reasons. First, I have long been aware that modern bishops or equivalent church leaders, because of the size of their geographical area of responsibility and the multiplicity of the demands made of them, could not hope to get close enough to clergy and their families to know them intimately as a pastor. Pastors' families in particular are often a neglected area of pastoral care in the church. By being freed from wider administrative responsibilities, I had the time and space to develop a pastoral role with the families of the clergy and ministers. Second, I had no authority and no jurisdiction. This had both advantages and disadvantages. On the one hand, since I was not a "line manager" for clergy and ministers, I could receive their confidences with the assurance that whatever was confided remained with me unless the person concerned requested me to take it elsewhere. Discipline remained with the churches. The lack of a given authority, on the other hand, could be a handicap when decisions were needed quickly without having to await denominational approvals.

The role of chief pastor requires the church leader to know and care about what is happening in the congregations and parishes committed to his or her care. For this I had the benefit of the Denominational Relations Group, an advisory group of senior clergy, each representing one of the denominations, who could both tell me what was happening and advise and suggest courses of action. There were also other gatherings of people, both ordained and lay, with whom it was possible to share in leadership in the churches. Having long advocated collaborative ministry, I was more than happy to take advantage of every possible way of sharing the ministry of ecumenical moderator with others. The idea of the "bishop in council" envisaged by the Swindon Report and the *Baptism, Eucharist and Ministry* report very greatly influenced me in the practice of personal, collegial and communal *episkopé* in my ministry as ecumenical moderator.

Expectations of the role of the ecumenical moderator varied according to denominational background. Anglicans treated me as they would their bishop.

Anglican diocesan and area bishops made a particular point of handing me their pastoral staff when I was giving the blessing at events at which they were present. For Methodists I was a circuit minister with responsibilities usually exercised by the chairman of the district, but the legal power still lay in the hands of the circuit superintendent. The United Reformed Church District Council took my position seriously enough to regard me as their moderator-in-residence and to invite me to induct two ministers to pastorates in the city. Baptists accepted me as a senior Baptist minister, and some consulted me as they would their general superintendent. For Roman Catholics my office was an enigma. There was no possibility of the bishop handing on to me any of his authority, but he did appeal to Catholics in the Deanery to recognize my position and make of it what they could. In practice I was warmly welcomed to participate in many events, and my presence on the Deanery Pastoral Council and the Diocesan Ecumenical Commission was not only welcomed, but sought.

In an area with such close ecumenical co-operation, the churches other than the Roman Catholic Church practised joint confirmation, whereby people were initiated to communicant church membership through the laying-on by hands of representatives of the denominations involved in the ecumenical parish concerned. In the present state of church non-unity, it was always essential that each denomination be visibly represented; and since it was not appropriate for the laying-on of hands to be given by the ecumenical moderator, I either presided at the eucharist or preached on these occasions. The same was true of inductions of ministers: the appropriate officer of the church concerned would carry out the induction, while I was always asked to represent the whole Christian community in welcoming the new minister and often to preach. Though not permitted to induct ministers, except by the United Reformed Church, I was always involved in some appropriate way with the selection and appointment of ordained and lay people to parochial and other salaried appointments.

Some reflections
Out of the first five years of this pioneering post, several matters arose which seem to me to require some further thought.

1. Geographical area of function
It is very important to recognize that geography is significant. My area of responsibility was co-extensive with the boundaries of the Borough of Milton Keynes. While these borders did not exactly match those of any of the churches involved, they were the borders of the secular authority. It was the area of the human community, 19.3 x 9.7 km. (12 x 6 miles) – an area similar to that considered in the Swindon Report.

Milton Keynes Borough incorporates two Anglican deaneries, a major part of a Roman Catholic deanery, most of a Methodist circuit, a small United Reformed Church district and the grouping of a number of Baptist churches in fellowship. The size was significant because it was manageable from the point of view of the ecumenical moderator, who had to relate to 66 congregations and their ordained and lay leadership.

As I approached my task, I realized something of how effective for leadership was the early church experience of the city bishop, the chief pastor for the city. On this pattern the secular boundaries determine the church's area of influence, which makes eminent sense from the point of view of the missionary nature of the church. Not only was I able to relate to the congregations committed to my care, but I could be seen by them at more frequent intervals than church leaders with much greater areas of pastoral care.

For the secular authorities as well as the other faith communities, the ecumenical moderator could be identified as the leader of the Christian community – which was much easier than having to deal with several Christian leaders, each representing a different church.

At the same time, the denominational church leaders for the area were able to entrust their people into the care of the ecumenical moderator, while not losing any part of their authority or jurisdiction, which are so important.

The area of responsibility suggested in the 1997 report from Wales, *Towards the Making of an Ecumenical Bishop in Wales*, is slightly smaller than that of either Swindon or Milton Keynes. It has the advantage of including several local ecumenical projects (LEPs). While it is a good place to start, the danger is that it could very easily be sidelined by the participating traditions, with no possibility of anything similar being done anywhere else.

2. No authority, no jurisdiction

The day my appointment was announced I received an urgent phone call from one of the church leaders, who had seen the press release announcing the appointment, which was headlined "A bishop in all but name". "You do realize," he said, "that you have no authority and no jurisdiction." I was pleased to be able to assure my colleague that I fully understood and accepted that I had to earn any authority I might have, and that there was no question of my having jurisdiction over anyone or anything.

In the post-apostolic period a number of models of bishop existed.[1] One model was that of the overseer for a group of congregations meeting in a city and the surrounding countryside. Each would have its presbyter, but the symbol of unity, the president at the eucharist, was the bishop. It was in those terms that I saw the role of the ecumenical moderator – a symbol of unity without legal authority, but drawing his or her authority from the local eucharistic community and therefore to be respected as representing the whole community. "No authority and no jurisdiction" meant just that: without legal power and without given authority. Others saw this, too, including a Catholic priest who said to me, "You are our bishop," meaning simply the local Christian leader whose authority lay elsewhere than in law or power.

Towards the Making of an Ecumenical Bishop in Wales indicates that the proposed ecumenical bishop will have certain authority vested in him by the participating churches, each giving him such authority as it can. The absence of the Roman Catholic Church as a partner in the Covenant and the fact that the Church in Wales (Anglican) is free of the legal constraints of the Church of England mean that more authority is possible for the ecumenical bishop than was the case for the ecumenical moderator of Milton Keynes, or would have been for the ecumenical bishop of Swindon.

3. For the sake of unity

The foundation documents for the Milton Keynes Christian Council in its search for what became the ecumenical moderator reveal that considerable effort went into finding the appropriate title. By contrast, the Swindon Report decided, after careful discussion, to use the term "bishop", noting that "since some think that episcopacy is essential, the rest of us choose to accept a bishop in Thamesdown and District for the sake of unity and mission".

Milton Keynes began with the term "pastoral president", then explored other possibilities – among them "prefect" and "praepositus" (a commander, something to be preferred, but also "not absolutely good" according to Cassell's Dictionary!). In the end "ecumenical moderator" was chosen. While this solved the problem of the opposing expectations of episcopal and non-episcopal, my own experience was that it often had to be interpreted both within and outside church circles – and when that happened, the simplest explanation was "a bishop for all the churches", so that "bishop" might just as well have been chosen for the title.

In Swindon the non-episcopal traditions had been prepared to accept the term bishop – "for the sake of unity and mission". My guess is that this was possible because all the traditions involved had experience of some form of personal *episkopé*, although under a variety of names and with varying degrees of authority. Congregationally ordered traditions and those with a presbyterian order have the greatest difficulties with the concept. What is significant is that in Swindon and in Milton Keynes there was a willingness to accept the practice – with or without the term – "for the sake of unity and mission".

The report from Wales shows no hesitation about the use of the term bishop, even though several non-episcopally ordered churches are participants in the Covenant. This grows out of the work done in producing the 1986 report, *Ministry in a Uniting Church: From Recognition to Reconciliation*. While the report itself was not implemented, all the responses from the churches said they could live with the concept of a bishop. The subsequent ten years of reflection and conversation on covenanting reflected a recognition that they would have to come to terms with episcopacy.[2]

4. Personal episkopé

BEM pointed to the exercise of ordained ministry in a *personal, collegial* and *communal* way (Ministry, para. 26), and this includes the exercise of episcopal ministry.

The Swindon Report came down on the side of a bishop-in-council, noting that the churches involved were quite clear about their desire to have a bishop. At the same time, they recognized the *communal episkopé* of the proposed Mission Council as being necessary to complement the *personal episkopé* of the bishop. There was also mention of each being a check to possible excesses in the other.

The Milton Keynes experiment provided for *personal* and *communal episkopé* working alongside each other and went further than Swindon on the third element named by *BEM*, *collegial episkopé*. The ecumenical moderator was a member of the Presidency of the Christian Council, and shared his oversight with the Denominational Relations Group and his ministry with the ordained clergy throughout the borough. The communal *episkopé* in Milton Keynes was exercised by the Assembly of the Milton Keynes Christian Council, acting through its Executive. My experience was that this arrangement worked well.

The Welsh Covenanting Churches in their report propose a bishop-in-council, bringing together *personal* and *communal episkopé*. Unlike Milton Keynes, there is no presidency, but the ecumenical bishop will enjoy *collegiality* with church leaders in each participating denomination who exercise some form of personal *episkopé*. Wales goes further than Milton Keynes could in providing for the consecration of the ecumenical bishop. Although the Welsh report refers to the formation of Mission Council, no provision is made in the draft order of service for the commissioning of members of the Mission Council at the consecration of the ecumenical bishop. This omission will no doubt be dealt with later on.

One further difference between the Welsh proposal and the English experiences is that the Welsh report makes no specific reference to the ecumenical bishop as a "focus of unity", although this might be construed from the description of the bishop's role (section 10). *Personal* ecumenical *episkopé* must necessarily incorporate some idea of the focus of unity, since this is fundamental to the concept of personal *episkopé* as it has been practised and experienced through the centuries.

In conclusion

While I am grateful to God for the privilege of having been allowed to serve in this unusual and pioneering post, I believe that there must be development of the idea of ecumenical *episkopé*. The Swindon Report was a useful starting point; the Milton Keynes experiment took the idea into a practical application; the document produced by the Covenanting Churches in Wales breaks new ground. Can this consultation provide the basis for further experimentation, and a wider application of the principle of ecumenical oversight, during the transitional period in which the churches are not organically united, as in the case of the Church of South India and its fellow united churches?

NOTES

[1] Cf. J. Zizioulas, "Episkopé and Episkopos in the Early Church", in *Episkopé and Episcopate in Ecumenical Perspective*, Geneva, WCC, 1974, pp.31-42.

[2] Cf. *Ministry in a Uniting Church*, Swansea, Commission of the Covenanted Churches, 1986, esp. pp.28-31.

6. THE DISTAFF OF GOD: SOME REFLECTIONS ON A NEW EPISCOPATE

Penny Jamieson

When I was asked to contribute a paper to this volume, I was uneasy. Was it, I wondered, a variation on the theme of being an interesting exhibit – a consequence of my episcopacy that I have not relished? In fact, beyond being what I am, a bishop who is a woman, much of what I do is the same as my male colleagues. I answer letters, go to meetings (too many), arrange appointments, drive too far too fast, put out fires and so on. The pitfalls are also the same: I overwork, I get tired and irritable, I forget things, including my prayers. It feels very ordinary, and I wondered what I had of substance to offer.

What I can offer is not graced by years of experience, nor with any depth of philosophical or theological expertise. Since I have been ordained, all my theological reflection has necessarily been so closely woven with the fabric of my ministry that it has been done, if not on the hoof or on my knees, often in long and intense discussion, generally with other women. What I offer in this paper is quite simply a somewhat tentative and provisional ramble through my reflections on these first years of my episcopate. I cannot promise anything of significant profundity or novelty, but it is the fruit of a unique if brief experience. These are the reflections of a novice, and the story is of necessity a personal story.

In many ways, these have been the most difficult years of my life, but if there is one thing I have learned very clearly it is the relationship between prayer, experience and theological reflection. When, almost immediately following my ordination to the episcopate, I found myself thrown into a maelstrom of confusion, anger and at times downright rebellion, it was these that provided, often in uneasy and imbalanced proportions, the framework for my return to both sanity and an acceptance of my vocation.

In part, the turmoil I experienced was due to being taken by surprise. I honestly had not expected ever to be a bishop. While I do not think that my male colleagues have been especially ambitious in this regard, it was for them within the realms of possibility. For me, it was beyond the reach of imagination. All too often, it would seem, our vision, the exact shape and nature of vocation as we perceive it, is tempered by the available possibilities. God's vision is larger.

So I cannot pretend that I was ready and waiting for this call. Indeed, I was quite resistant. This was contrary to my earlier experience. When I had sought ordination as a priest, the late Edward Norman, then Bishop of Wellington, was very hesitant. It took me a long time to persuade the church of the validity of my call. When the church wanted to make me a bishop, it took the church some time to convince me. I am a reluctant prophet.

All I know about episcopacy, I know in this context: this place, Aotearoa New Zealand, in particular this diocese of Dunedin; and this time, when like the Anglican Church in many other parts of the world, we are experiencing very rapid and profound changes – in the shape of our ministry, in adaptation to financial constraints, in the revision of liturgy and patterns of worship, and in relations between the church that is the successor of the colonists and the church of our indigenous minority, to name just a few. For the time being, however, the initiation of change is, as far as I can tell, behind us, and I trust we are now entering a period of consolidation. My election and consecration to the episcopate should be seen in this context.

At the time of my consecration – a time of unprecedented excitement, even hype in this diocese, fueled by enthusiasm and response on a worldwide scale – I was frequently asked, microphones thrust into my face, "What is the difference between a male bishop and a female one?" Well, apart from the obvious, which I can only assume they knew, I really did not know. Indeed, I knew all too little of what a bishop's calling entailed. It soon became apparent that I would learn only in the place of my consecration and with the people for whom I was bishop. So I set out immediately to get to know the place, the people, their history, their hopes, all that they were proud of and wanting to tell me; and to learn also to listen to the silences, to what they could not readily share. I wanted, by the grace of God, to bind myself into their life, to graft my story and that of my family onto the story of these people, with whom I had been placed in this very particular relationship. It was the beginnings of affection, and it is an essential ingredient of all Christian ministry. I knew this grafting would take time, and so I made a resolution not to travel outside the country for at least two years.

The provinces of Otago and Southland (which made up the diocese of Dunedin) were settled in the middle of the 19th century, largely by Scottish people of the Free Church persuasion. Anglicanism here has always been a minority Christian denomination, squashed theologically and politically speaking between our two major sister denominations, Presbyterians and Roman Catholics. Anglicans here have been fiercely defensive of their own identity. Like the Episcopal Church in Scotland (we have a companion relationship with the diocese of Edinburgh), the church is popularly reckoned to have taken its defining identity from Anglo-Catholicism, though as in all New Zealand dioceses this particular identity has been tempered by the broad, middle-ground of "churchmanship" that is so common in this country.

This is predominantly a rural diocese, situated at the southern end of a long thin country. Geographically it is the largest; in terms of population it is one of the two smallest. Our two major cities, Dunedin and Invercargill, with a population of 90,000 and 50,000 respectively, are small by comparison with other cities. The population of the area has been slowly but steadily declining since the days of the gold rush at the end of the 19th century, when Dunedin was the largest city in New Zealand. We have many very small country churches which have never had a resident priest. Many of our parishes consist of four, five, or six churches, and the priest has to develop skills in low-flying in order to meet their Sunday needs. In effect, the definition of parish with which we operate (though this is about to change) is the number of churches which together can raise sufficient funds to meet the stipend, or part-stipend, of a priest. We have 34 priests in parish ministry and 86 churches, a few of which do not really know whether they are still open or not.

Episcopally, the diocese had a very steady history until after the second world war. Samuel Tarrant Nevill's initial episcopacy of 49 years established this sense of steadiness. The fifth bishop, Walter Robinson (1969-74), espoused the cause of church union, then a very live debate within the country, but there were deep divisions within the diocese, and when he died suddenly and prematurely in office, the sense of guilt was unbearable. His successor (and my predecessor) Peter Mann was bishop for 14 years and did much to re-establish that sense of steady stability that has been the hallmark of this diocese.

Perhaps because of its small number of priests, the diocese of Dunedin has often – and always since the 1930s – selected its bishops from beyond its own borders. In that respect I was no different from my predecessors. I am also, in my personal history and piety though not by party persuasion, more than loosely identified with historical Anglo-Catholicism. In these respects my election was not the sudden departure with tradition that the obvious change in gender led many people to believe.

I also learned very early on that one of the unarticulated agendas in electing a bishop from one of the northern dioceses derives from a fear of isolation and a longing to retain and redevelop connections with the rest of our rapidly changing church. The relatively "high" doctrine of episcopacy that is common here makes it natural to look to the bishop to give effect to this. This uneasy quest for change, balanced against a very steady, largely traditional Anglicanism and a measure of insecurity, makes this a difficult place in which to both justify and effect change.

There were thus two dimensions to episcopacy that challenged me, the universal and the local. The first I sensed as a call both to help this diocese find and cherish its place in our church and to hold out a vision of church and of God which could, if graced, help to expand the hearts of God's people. The second challenged me to develop pastoral skills that would enable me to care for and challenge the church in this diocese, to find the link between pastoral practice and spiritual reality, and to work creatively and co-operatively on the mission of the church. Poised in the middle, so to speak, I searched for the connections.

I have always and increasingly had a strong affection for a theology of church that talks of the Body of Christ, with distinct parts fulfilling different functions. This speaks to me of both our interdependency, our need for each other, and of the gift of communion (*koinonia*). As Christ daily, weekly, links his resurrection life with ours through the sacrament of his body and blood, so we are linked with all others with whom he is also linked by the same sacrament. "We are the body of Christ", and Christ is the head of the body. The spiritual life of each one of us as individuals is enormously important, but it finds its authenticity, its way to God, through the lived and linked life with other Christians, sacramentally and scripturally. John Donne wrote that "No 'man' is an island", and that is as true of the spiritual life as of any other part of human life.

But Christian communities can easily and quite intentionally become turned in on themselves. I have come to see that one of the gifts of episcopacy to the church is that the vision of a life beyond the community's own congregational life is embodied in a person. Through the flesh and blood person of the bishop, who connects them with each other and with the wider church, there is a glimpse, however fragmented, of what it means to be part of the church universal. And this call reaches beyond: a further aspect of a bishop's ministry is to lift the church into the heart of God.

I have been astonished by how much of this happens simply because the bishop is the bishop. Is this what is meant by the grace of orders?, I wonder. But as in all exercise of priesthood, the dangerous opportunity is ever present of attracting the focus onto ourselves rather than onto the God we serve. This is especially an issue for women priests and bishops, particularly when the novelty of our appointment draws attention to ourselves. A kenotic, self-emptying spirituality both engages and informs my desire to know when to stand aside.

I have found that it is continually necessary to point to the vision beyond; to be as transparent as I can about my own faith and my own relation with God – not only from the shelter of the pulpit, but at all levels of my functioning and relating episcopally. This is not always easy for an essentially private person, but with integrity and prayer, some modest approximation can be made.

So when we are talking about how we might change, adapt to or live with the practices of the church at large, I endeavour to articulate, constantly and repeatedly, the reasons for this in the terms of the faith by which we all live. We are not just changing for the sake of change nor are we changing because things have changed "up north", but just as each person, each parish, does not stand alone, neither does this diocese. We will as appropriate and necessary be prepared to make changes.

In no issue has this been more clearly required of us than in consenting and adapting to the new constitution of the church. This gives equal partnership to all sections of the church: Pakeha (immigrant and of immigrant descent), Maori (the indigenous people of these islands) and Polynesian (the Diocese of Polynesia, the islands of the South Pacific situated to the north of New Zealand). Located as we are at the southern end of the country, the Diocese of Dunedin does not have a very large Maori population, which makes it very difficult for our people to grasp the implications of the church's commitment to a partnership with the Maori. For instance we are required to share our financial resources (all too little at the best of times) with a minority we can hardly see, and with whom it is not easy to form real relations; but this must be done.

The church also reaches beyond this country, and the people of this diocese have enjoyed this. Within the wider Anglican communion I have had some role in the development of understanding of women's episcopal vocation and ministry, I rejoice that there are now more of us to share this role, for it could easily become a major distraction both to the practical working out of what I understand about this ministry and to simply doing the job God has called me to do.

Locally, I have also found the theological base for my ministry within the theology of the whole and the parts of the Pauline doctrine of the Body of Christ. The traditional roles of the bishop as shepherd of the flock, teacher of the faith and focus of unity tend to coalesce in the light of experience and of prayer and find focus in my growing awareness of the bishop as "spiritual director" for the diocese; that is through prayer, and making rigorous links between prayer and practice, lifting the church into the heart of God. There are many ways this can happen; here I can mention only a few which relate to some of the significant issues I have faced.

These are the days of increasing congregational isolation in all dioceses and across all denominations in this country. In part, this reflects our churches' struggle within an increasingly individualistic and anti-institutional society. And there is constantly the pressure of not enough money. It is no wonder that parishes resist attempts by a central body to shape their life; and because at times they are fragile and untrusting, they resist attempts to help them. I have found that I must articulate a sense of diocesan unity that does not seek to compel our parishes or to distort the particularity of their place and their piety, but constantly gives practical respect to both their individuality and their place within the family of the diocese.

This is not always easy. A recent example is our approach to Christian giving. For some time now, this diocese has been living in some fear about facing up to the reality not only of our parlous financial situation but also of the basic Christian call to generosity. Our God is a generous God; how can we but respond, if we are to live an authentic Christian life?

A small working group found that almost every parish realized that it was slipping up in this regard, but none knew how to tackle the problem. Such is the general resistance to diocesan directives that it would have been pointless to have initiated a diocesan programme. Yet it was a clearly acknowledged diocesan problem. So the working group set about trying to hold these opposites in tension (something I have always thought Anglicans are naturally quite good at).

What the working group came up with was a surprising response to the seemingly opposite requirements of the situation. The group produced an enormous folder of resources of all types, serious, sermonic, practical and humorous – far more than any parish could take on at one go. So, if a parish was going to take part in the venture – and participation was not "required" – it had to choose, to consider carefully its own practice and piety, what would work and what would give offence. In effect, participation entailed taking responsibility – not, as with so many diocesan ventures, by providing parishes with someone to blame. The other side of the paradox, the clear need of most of our parishes for support, was attended to by the diocese's agreeing through synod (not the best way, but the only way we have) that in the period between Easter and Ascension parishes would, if they wished, make one Sunday the focus of their programme. In this way each parish had a choice, but the facilitating of more or less simultaneous activity within the parishes would create a sense of mutual solidarity and support, a sense of not being alone, of being part of the Body.

In these days there is much talk about inclusiveness, especially about inclusive language. While our new New Zealand Prayer Book has made significant advances in that respect, our hymnology is for the most part woefully retarded. Theologically, the move towards inclusiveness is sound; God is utterly undiscriminating, and although our prejudices always get in our way and limit our response, we can do no less than be constantly ready and willing to stretch ourselves to include all of God's people. Our language should both enable and reflect this. But from where I stand, the primary issue is that of an inclusivity of the heart, an embrace that seeks to be wider, that is constantly willing to be stretched, that does not hide behind dogma, new or old, but which knows the joy and the demand of love. Inclusivity of language, yes, but also of liturgy and life.

In practical and human terms this is far more than any of us can accomplish; but no matter, for it is a dimension of the church, of the Body of Christ, and in this respect we are not alone. For my part, as bishop, I have been both surprised and humbled at how my office has given me a profile from which I can widen and expand the vision of what the church could be and who might find a place within it. Boundaries have expanded, and the embrace has widened. This is not a personal attribute; it is a function of what I am, at this time and in this place.

It is my perception that when I was elected, the diocese was seeking not only novelty or a new kind of link to the rest of the church, but also to give expression to a desire for a new style of leadership. Essentially and explicitly, the people were seeking a more consultative style of leadership. As institutions go out of fashion, so do the hierarchies that keep the common life of those institutions on course. The church is no different from other areas of New Zealand life in this respect. In recent years, the consultative style of leadership has come to be associated with women's ways of working. Many women's organizations and groups have indeed experimented with and refined consensus models of decision-making – some with notable success, others with equally notable lack of success.

Beyond a general desire for the development of a consultative style of leadership, I am not sure just what the expectations were. I am equally sure that no one person in this diocese had the same idea as any other. So, although I do have – and have had through my ordained life – a commitment to such a style, I also had a problem. Several of my male colleagues also hold these ideals – how could it be otherwise if they were both to respond and relate to the aspirations of the contemporary church? And some of them are very good at it. Because I am a woman, it is both expected that I should operate consultatively and noticed when I do not, when I get into the "boss" mode. My male colleagues do not have the same high level of visibility and critique in this regard.

One significant lesson I have had to grasp here is patience. It takes far more time to operate consultatively in a diocese than in a parish, because a diocese is much larger and more diffuse in both people and area. Communications in a diocese become enormously important, for there is a constant need to open things up and to avoid operating in little groups that seem inaccessible and threatening to other people. But I have also learned that there is a need to repeat continually, on every possible occasion and in as many different places and ways possible, the thematic content of the message I wish to get across, for no amount of communication is enough and I can always expect to fall short in this regard.

Apart from our annual diocesan synod, we have no formal method of decision-making by consultation. And synod is itself a bewildering and even an alienating experience for most people. So although formal consent might be achieved, the level at which decisions are owned by the people, the priests and the parishes of our diocese is very low indeed. Hence there is motivation to develop less formal lines of consultation. This we have done by making each of our three archdeaconries into area deaneries, so that greater contact is achieved between clergy and laity in groups that are manageable both by size and geography. By meeting regularly with archdeacons, the area deans, we have gained greater contact and ability to share information and resources across the whole diocese. It is important, I have discovered, that the contact be not only with myself, in a one-to-one forum, but also a shared opportunity for people to listen to each other. In that process we can all begin, by the grace of the Holy Spirit of God working among us, to discern the direction we are called to follow together. It is also necessary if we are to give some practical, livable expression to the theological dictum that oversight belongs to the whole church which the bishop holds on its behalf.

There are some snags. When consultation begins to take root, I have found that anxiety levels can rise. I think there are several reasons for this. In the first place, it appears that some measure of responsibility is being handed over. Indeed, it is; for if people are listened to both by me and by their colleagues they feel the need to become more responsible in what they say. The process is necessarily somewhat circular: as ideas shape up, I feed them back to get more insight. Anxiety arises if people do not know where the final responsibility for the decision-making lies. This dynamic is especially strong when it is clear that there is no common mind. I have found that it is necessary for me, where appropriate, to take this responsibility unambiguously; while I may receive blame, I must not get into the routine of blame and counter-blame that frequently follows such action. This means of course that I must be able to hold my ground without resorting to self-defence. I try to maintain a steady, non-anxious presence, which is not always easy.

This leads into what I want to say about authority, which is probably the most difficult issue for bishops in Aotearoa New Zealand to address. Issues of power, control and authority are at the heart of the current critique of episcopacy, to which the call for more consultative styles of leadership is central. It is all too easy under such pressure to act out of dogma: "Of course bishops have power; that is what we are here for; and if people do not like it, they had better move out!" Or, at the opposite end of the scale: "Bishops do not have any power; the real power lies in the community and we just do what they ask us to do." In my experience neither is true, and both are dangerous. Power exercised *de haut en bas*, unrelationally, will never take root, just as bad decisions by a synod do not take root. In fact, the dynamic is very similar. But on the other hand it is nonsense to say that as bishops we have no power. We clearly do, as is shown by the rise in the level of anxiety when people think we are going to back off or when a diocese is between episcopates. The issue is rather one of being honest about what power we do have, of being responsible in its use and of being open to the point of transparency about how we use it. Sometimes some real paradoxes have emerged; for one, it has not been uncommon for me to insist on consultation. The ironies do not go unnoticed.

I have found that it is essential for me to remember that any authority, any power I have has been entrusted to me by the church for the benefit of the church. The basis of any effective use of any power, in my experience, is establishing and maintaining good, sound relationships. It takes a long time to build up trust, and that trust can never be presumed upon. Every time I visit Anglican dioceses here or abroad which are larger than this one, I thank God that if I had to be a bishop, it is here. In a diocese of this size it is possible to build those relationships and to keep them intact. This is essential, even as priorities change over time.

When I reflect on what I do, using the opportunities that my experience as a woman offers to me, it seems to me that I am seeking to make space – "wombspace", if you like – in which others can grow and experience the life-giving power of the Spirit. Often I feel that, as in pregnancy, I am "holding the space"; by my attitude and responses and not least by my prayer, I am, in a non-anxious mode, holding the boundary, defining that space as unambivalently Christian and as intentionally within the church. This is particularly significant in times of potential controversy, as when one of our priests died from an AIDS-related illness, or when a promising ordinand went awry and there were calls for instant cancellation of the status of ordinand. The one needed safe space to die; the other needed safe space to discern the meaning of vocation. In both instances, it seemed to me that providing such space was uniquely both the function and the privilege of the bishop. For "wombspace" is like "sheepfold"; each is an image of both enclosure and room for growth. An ancient image of episcopacy is reborn.

These issues and others have preoccupied me during these years. They have undoubtedly had an impact on me spiritually. I think that ordination always changes people – that is what the Holy Spirit is about – but for me it has been a sea-change. My consecration precipitated me into a realm of activity, publicity and spiritual turmoil for which, despite my best efforts beforehand, I was totally unprepared. The ordinal itself is quite terrifying in the expectations that it gives rise to, but these pale into insignificance against the expectations that people had of me. I coined the word "iconized" for that experience: I felt that I was being made into an icon, a symbol created to hold the hopes, the dreams, the fears and the frustrations of the people.

My very humanity felt threatened; and I began a long and painful struggle – always, to my amazement, from the inside of faith – to find the match between the expectations of the church, people and sacrament, and myself. What was the real shape of episcopacy for me? There were some moments of severe doubt; but God knew what God was getting, even if, as it sometime seemed, no one else did.

I searched long and hard for the key to matching my interior life with my exterior life; specifically to matching the interior life of my spirit, all that I was and all that I longed to be for the God I had been called to serve, with the exterior life, in which all my relationships with friends, family, passing acquaintances and unknown strangers had shifted. It may seem facile to say in this day and age, but when the struggle was over and I had truly accepted my vocation, I saw that I had found that match through the somewhat dated, but enormously powerful mechanism of obedience. I cannot recommend it too highly.

I have often reflected on biblical analogies for all this, and there are many. One which is particularly resonant for me is the Book of Job. Like most such analogies, is has the ring of too much ease, but there are some points of contact. There were times when my plight seemed like an inexplicable and somewhat playful wager between God and Satan; there were times when it seemed to be doing no good to anyone around me; there were times when I cursed the day of my consecration; there were "friends" who told me that not only was what I was doing wrong, but also that

I was wrong (they, like Job's friends, were of course unambiguously "right"); there were times when I was very angry. I found that my perception of the plight of others in similar circumstances was deepened; and I grew through this to a strong sense of appreciation of the utterly unassailable "God" of God, and I did put most trust unreservedly in my God.

It is a truth of the spiritual life that our experiences, even our pain and struggles, are not given to us for ourselves alone. There was for me a darkness, a profound sense of the absence of God; this is not an uncommon feeling, but I have found that radical insecurity is a place where God is to be found.

The fundamental spiritual issue became the conversion of the faithful. Both within the church and on the boundaries are many who seek, from within faith, to regrasp the significance and intensity of a commitment already made. For these people, lay and ordained, it is the question of the call within the call. Such questions arise especially sharply at times of transition.

The quest for a spirituality of transition arises when people enter the ordained ministry, a time of profound transition. With ordination come immediate external changes – in dress, in the way people function in the liturgy, in their relations with the community, in their public life and also within their family. The task for all the newly-ordained is to seek that match between their exterior life and their interior life. The intensity of this task diminishes as time passes, but not its imperative.

And the Christian community is also in profound and confusing transition. The soul of the church cries out for leaders who will eschew triumphalism, listen to the reality of the questions and the pain, and journey alongside the people in the darkness that is the gift of God. Is all this new, or is it as old as the call of God to humankind, and what does it anticipate?

The early reports of the Eames Commission, the Archbishop of Canterbury's Commission on Communion and Women in the Episcopate, used the word "provisional" of women's orders. Many women and not a few men found this term thoroughly offensive, implying as it does that women's orders are of a temporary nature. I would like to conclude by offering an alternative understanding of "pro-visional". As is well known, women's orders, whether to the priesthood or the episcopate, are not universally acknowledged throughout the Anglican communion. It is both my belief and my experience that this fragility and insecurity, far from being an affront, are quite precious. We women cannot presume on the institutional church as our male colleagues can, and we therefore remain steadily "off-centre" and correspondingly closer to those on the boundary. We are also spared, if we have the grace to grasp the opportunity, some of the spiritual and personal traps of excessive institutionalization.

But more than that, I believe women's orders are truly pro-visionary in the sense of anticipatory, even prophetic, calling and re-calling both us and the whole church of God to a lived and experienced faithfulness, calling us all to accept radical insecurity as gift and not to presume on our orders, for the gift of the Spirit is just that, a gift and never a right. So I thank God for the gift of "pro-visionality"; it is indeed a gift from women to the whole of church of God.

7. THREE GAMES IN A LONG ECUMENICAL SET

Leuenberg, Meissen and Porvoo on Ministry and *Episkopé*

Martin H. Cressey

This paper was written in Northern Ireland while on voluntary service with the Corrymeela community. That context has affected its style. For one thing, I did not have with me my set of bilateral and multilateral reports; so I wrote out of my basic impressions rather than detailed re-scrutiny of texts. More important, I was in a place where ecumenism is both more necessary and more suspect than in my home base in Cambridge; so only the essentials of the hierarchy of truths press upon the consciousness.

My title, drawing an analogy with tennis, reflects both a sense that the issues surrounding ministry and *episkopé* have often been treated as a theological "sport", and the fact that although the ecumenical discussion has been in process for a long time, the end of the set, much more the end of the match, still seems distant.

I was personally involved in the Leuenberg conversations as one of the Reformed participants, struggling with my first experience of ecumenical work in a language not my own and later, with others, at the task of translating the text into English. It was salutary to realize that the issues which had divided Lutheran and Reformed in German-speaking Europe and made the path of church union in Germany a difficult one were not easy even to state in English. I used to sit next to a Finnish Lutheran bishop. Coming, as it were, from the opposite margins of the European Reformation, we were often at one in bewilderment at the intensity of discussion around battle slogans like "*manducatio impiorum*".

Yet on ministry and *episkopé* there was fairly rapid consensus, since all agreed that the constitutional form of church life was secondary to the doctrines of justification, sanctification, Word and sacraments. I was frequently reminded of how the founders of the London Missionary Society affirmed that the purpose of "sending the glorious gospel of the blessed God" was consonant with a variety of ecclesiological and ministerial structures, whose formation could be left to the newly emergent churches of converts, according to their own civil polities and cultures. Even the hesitations expressed by representatives of the Scandinavian Lutheran churches at the time of entering into the Leuenberg agreement were in terms of the difficulty of securing the necessary parliamentary permission in their countries rather than in terms of episcopal order.

Thus the Leuenberg agreement and the deepened fellowship to which it has led for such a wide range of Reformation churches in Europe and beyond represents for me a pragmatic approach to ministry and *episkopé*. Whatever the origins of the Ignatian episcopate, the development of diocesan bishops as the leaders and pastors of the church in Europe can be seen as the expression in church terms of a leadership pattern produced by the adaptation of Roman political order to the needs of the church, first in post-imperial chaos and then in the new pattern of national states. At the Reformation the episcopal order was continued, modified or radically changed. To find a way back to visible unity certainly requires constructive thought and action, but it should be based on response to the needs of evangelism and service.

In the context of the search in the 1970s for an inter-church covenant in England, it was possible for my own church, the United Reformed Church, to contemplate an extension into its regional structure of the pattern familiar locally; just as the local church had a church meeting of all the members, a corporate leadership of elders, of whom the minister was one, and a personal and pastoral role for the minister, so there could be roles for a synod of lay and ministerial members, appropriate committees and a ministerial moderator in each of twelve provinces. These moderators would in the long term have become bishops, reconciled in order with the bishops of the Church of England, but the URC strongly insisted that the covenant should begin with a partnership of regional oversight ministries with different historical origins. This proposal, which met some resistance even in the URC, was for the Church of England one of the major obstacles to covenanting.

The Meissen agreement between the Church of England and the Evangelical Church in Germany (EKD) marks an important advance. Here the bilateral dialogue is between two comprehensive national churches. For the Church of England an episcopate in historical succession is a key factor in the possibility of that comprehensiveness. When the Anglican-Methodist unity scheme was discussed in the 1960s and 1970s, it was made clear that, while difference of theological views on the meaning of the episcopate was acceptable, an unvarying practice of episcopal ordination of ministers would be necessary to enable the two churches to unite. Thus the conversation with the EKD was complicated by the variety in forms of regional oversight in the various *Landeskirchen*. As an English Free Church minister, I looked carefully at the small print and footnotes to see how this complication had been handled. I am very glad to see and hear the working together of the Meissen partners – in particular the exchanges of episcopal visits and functions – but I also observe the restrictions still placed on sharing in ordinations, which have the effect of distinguishing the episcopal succession of Anglican orders from the varied patterns of ordination in Germany.

What then made the difference when the Anglican churches of Britain and Ireland together entered into conversation with Nordic and Baltic Lutheran churches? To a Reformed observer two factors seem to have been important. One was the fact that three of the four Anglican churches involved were not established churches – though in fairness it should be noted that the initiative in the whole matter came from the

Church of England. Since the Anglican-Presbyterian talks of the 1950s and 1960s, the first bilaterals of which I was theologically aware (as a Presbyterian ordinand), it has been clear to me that the Church of England and the Church of Scotland have always to struggle to distinguish their basic ecclesiologies from their social and political situations. The Episcopal Church of Scotland and the Presbyterian Church of England, the two minority and in that sense "free church" bodies, were often frustrated by their senior partners and at one point seriously considered "going it alone". The other and more important factor in the Porvoo process has been the fresh approach to understanding apostolic succession, in terms of a corporate succession of the whole church, expressed and focused, but neither guaranteed nor exhausted, by the succession in the episcopal sees.

It is the second factor which overcame the difficulty presented to Anglicans by the differences in historic circumstance between the continuity of the Swedish episcopate and the new beginning that had to be made in leadership of the Danish church, with consequences for Norway and Iceland also. Tactual succession of consecration is no longer seen in isolation as the sign of continuity; it is recognized that the intention in the presbyteral consecrations at the Reformation was to preserve the ordered continuity of the local churches, in the sense of the churches gathered round the bishops of the ancient Scandinavian dioceses.

Mary Tanner's presentation on the Porvoo agreement at the Sixth International Consultation of United and Uniting Churches (Ocho Rios, Jamaica, 1995) was welcomed, as would be expected from a consultation of churches of which some are episcopally ordered and all are in continuing conversations with episcopally ordered partner churches. Yet there remained an unease about how questions regarding *episkopé* are heard again and again in the quest for visible unity. The welcome and the unease come together in the recommendation of the Ocho Rios consultation to Faith and Order that it give:

> in its work on "ministry and authority"... special attention to the apostolicity of the whole church and its relation to the ministry of oversight expressed personally, collectively and communally, as well as the various means of safeguarding continuity in the life of the church.

Let me try to spell out what I think is the meaning of that debate among united churches, taking up points already noted in relation to Leuenberg, Meissen and Porvoo.

"Special attention to the apostolicity of the whole church" is sought by Ocho Rios because it is the key to the progress achieved in the Porvoo agreement. It is also the key to the understanding of the church of the Second Vatican Council, which, without departing from concepts of hierarchy and Petrine ministry, grounds its exposition of ecclesiology in the sense of the people of God as body of Christ and fellowship of the Spirit. As a Reformed teacher of systematic theology, I have found it a joy to be able to teach from the text of *Lumen Gentium* with a deep sense of shared understanding. On the other hand, I recall realizing on a first reading that Hans Küng's *The Church* was an uneven exposition of the *Lumen Gentium* approach precisely because it gave little attention to hierarchy. There is a tension between seeing apostolicity as primarily expressed in the wholeness of the church and seeing apostolicity as a wholeness which requires for its focussing a particular structure of ministry.

For some in the united churches Meissen raises the same kind of questions as arise from the difference between the South India and North India plans of union. In South India the existing ministries of the uniting churches were accepted – in the phrase culled from Wesley's hymn by Bishop Stephen Neill – "with undistinguishing regard". In North India a careful and complex process made it possible for the ministries to be so reconciled at the inception of the church that not only the united church itself but all its partner "mother" churches could recognize all the ministers of the new body from its very beginning. Yet the subsequent insistence by the Anglican communion on a "North India approach" seems to me to have been a major factor in the breakdown of schemes of union in Africa and Canada. The careful footnoting of Meissen still carries something which falls short of the South India declaration that all the uniting ministries are "real ministries of the Word and Sacraments in Christ's church, nor can any church say that the sacraments and other ministrations or ministries which he has blessed are invalid".[1]

So I am back at Leuenberg and the Augsburg Confession, to the basic conviction that it is enough to have agreement on the content of gospel preaching and the nature of meaning of the gospel sacraments of baptism and the Lord's supper – back also to the mission policy of the London Missionary Society:

> As the union of Christians of various denominations in carrying on this great work is a most desirable object, so, to prevent if possible any cause of future dissension, it is declared to be a fundamental principle of the Missionary Society that its design is not to send Presbyterianism, Independency, Episcopacy, or any other form of church order and government (about which there may be a difference of opinion among serious persons), but the glorious gospel of the blessed God to the heathen; and that it shall be left (as it ought to be left) to the minds of the persons whom God may call into the fellowship of his Son from among them to assume for themselves such a form of church government as to them shall appear most agreeable to the word of God.

That policy is more than the pragmatism of which I spoke earlier. It is a recognition of the diverse needs of peoples and cultures and of the diverse conclusions which may properly be drawn from the scriptures in meeting those needs. I declare myself entirely ready to be persuaded that in the next period and place of church life in which I serve (in my retirement) it may be seen to be good that a united church emerge with an episcopally ordered ministry. What I am not persuaded of is that there is any inevitability in that particular outcome of re-examining our traditions and searching the scriptures together.

So I end with a quotation from "The Reply of the Bishops of the Church of Sweden to the Lambeth Appeal" of 1920, brought recently to my attention by a retired bishop of the Church of North India:

> No particular organization of the church and of its ministry has been instituted *jure divino* – not even the order and discipline recorded in the New Testament. The Holy Scriptures vindicate the great principle of Christian freedom, unweariedly asserted by St Paul against all forms of legalistic religion. This great principle was applied with fresh strength and clearness by Martin Luther. But it was instituted by our Saviour himself, who, in taking leave of his disciples, did not regulate their future work by *a priori* rules or institutions, but directed them to the guidance of the Paraclete.[2]

NOTES

[1] Cf. Bengt Sundkler, *Church of South India: The Movement Towards Union*, London, Lutterworth, 1954, p.209.

[2] Cited in George Bell, *Documents on Christian Unity*, London, Oxford U.P., 1958, Vol. 1, p.185.

LIST OF PARTICIPANTS

Strasbourg, France
2 - 9 April 1997

Ms Evangelia AMOIRIDOU (Church of Greece), Aristoteleion University of Thessaloniki, Theological School, Department of Theology, 540 06 Thessaloniki, Greece

Rev. Neville CALLAM (Jamaica Baptist Union), 8 Haining Crescent, Kingston 5, Jamaica

Rev. Dr Donald CRAGG (Methodist Church of Southern Africa), P O Box 990508, Kibler Park 2053, South Africa

Rev. Martin CRESSEY (United Reformed Church), 147 Thornton Road, Girton, Cambridge CB3 0NE, England

Rev. Hugh CROSS (Baptist Union of Great Britain), 55 Slade Close, Ottery St Mary EX11 1SX, England

Rev. Dr Peter CROSS (Roman Catholic Church), St Francis Xavier Parish, 60 Davey Street, Frankston, Vic. 3199, Australia

Prof. John ERICKSON (Orthodox Church in America), St Vladimir's Seminary, 575 Scarsdale Road, Crestwood, NY 10707, USA

Prof. William FRANKLIN (Episcopal Church), General Theological Seminary, 175 Ninth Avenue, New York, NY 10010, USA

Rev. GAO Ying (China Christian Council), 2nd Area Bulg. ##1, An-hua-xi 11, Chao-yang District, Beijing 100 011, China (since 1999: Nanjing Theological Seminary, 17 Dajian Yinxiang, Shanghai Road, Nanjing 210 029, China)

Sister Dr Donna GEERNAERT s.c. (Roman Catholic Church), 90 Parent Avenue, Ottawa, Ontario K1N 7B1, Canada

Rev. Dr Daniell C. HAMBY (Episcopal Church), Consultation on Church Union, Research Park, 258 Wall Street, Princeton, NJ 08540-1514, USA

Rt Rev. John HIND (Church of England), Bishop's Lodge, Church Road, Worth, Crawley, West Sussex RH10 7RT, England

Rev. Dr Viorel IONITA (Romanian Orthodox Church), Conference of European Churches, 150, route de Ferney, 1211 Geneva 2, Switzerland

Bishop (Dr) Vassilios KARAYANNIS (Church of Cyprus), Holy Archbishopric, P O Box 1130, Nicosia, Cyprus

Bishop (Dr) MAXIMOS of Pittsburgh (Greek Orthodox Archdiocese of North and South America/ Ecumenical Patriarchate), 5201 Ellsworth Avenue, Pittsburgh, PA 15232-1421, USA

Rev. Farai D. MUZAREWA (Methodist Church), Private Bag 3002, Paulington, Mutare, Zimbabwe

Dr Elisabeth PARMENTIER (Evangelical Lutheran Church of Alsace and Lorraine), 3 rue du Herrenstein, 67330 Neuwiller-les-Saverne, France (part-time)

Rev. Prof. Martin PARMENTIER (Old Catholic Church), Burg. Lambooylaan 19, 1217 LB Hilversum, Netherlands

Prof. Dr Michael ROOT (Evangelical Lutheran Church in America), Institute for Ecumenical Research, 8 rue Gustave-Klotz, 67000 Strasbourg, France

Rev. Dr William G. RUSCH (Evangelical Lutheran Church in America), NCCCUSA/Faith and Order, Room 870, 475 Riverside Drive, New York, NY 10115-0050, USA

Rev. Jorge SCAMPINI (Roman Catholic Church), Albertinum, Square-des-Places 2, 1700 Fribourg, Switzerland

Rev. Dr Hazel SHERMAN (Baptist Union of Great Britain), Ashburn, Peppercorn Lane, Brecon, Powys LD3 9EG, Wales, Great Britain

Rev. Althea SPENCER-MILLER (Methodist Church), U.T.C.W.I., P O Box 136, 7 Golding Avenue, Kingston 7, Jamaica

Rt Rev. Stephen SYKES (Church of England), Bishop of Ely, Bishop's House, Ely, Cambridgeshire CB7 4DW, England

Dr Mary TANNER (Church of England), Council for Christian Unity, Church House, Great Smith Street, London SW1P 3NZ, England (since mid-1998: High Clere, Camp End Road, Weybridge KT13 0NW, England)

Rev. Jean TILLARD o.p. (Roman Catholic Church), Couvent Dominicain, 96 Avenue Empress, Ottawa, Ontario K1R 7G3, Canada

Prof. Dr Ola TJÖRHOM (Church of Norway), Faculty of Theology, School of Mission and Theology, Misjonsveien 34, 4024 Stavanger, Norway

Staff
Dr Peter BOUTENEFF, Executive Secretary
Rev. Dr Alan D. FALCONER, Director
Mrs Renate SBEGHEN, Administrative Assistant

Apologies
Those invited indicating their unability to attend and their wish to be informed of the results:

Prof. Anna-Marie AAGAARD, Denmark
Bishop BASIL of Sergievo, England
Dr Silke-Petra BERGJAN, Germany
Prof. Sven-Erik BRODD, Sweden
Prof. Dr Ingolf U. DALFERTH, Switzerland
Metropolitan DEMETRIOS of Vresthena, Greece
Prof. David A.S. FERGUSSON, Scotland
Prof. Dr Kyriaki FITZGERALD, Switzerland

Rev. Prof. Stanley HARAKAS, USA
Prof. Dr Eilert HERMS, Germany
Rt Rev. Dr Penelope JAMIESON, New Zealand
Bishop KALLISTOS of Diokleia, England
Bishop Rosemary KÖHN, Norway
Archhbishop Dr Mesrob KRIKORIAN, Austria
Rt Rev. Victoria MATTHEWS, Canada
Pröpstin Helga TRÖSKEN, Germany
Prof. Dr Dorothea WENDEBORG, Germany
Rt Rev. Rowan WILLIAMS, Wales

Crêt-Bérard, Switzerland
5 - 11 September 1997

Dr Kyriaki FITZGERALD (Greek Orthodox Archdiocese of North and South America/Ecumenical Patriarchate), USA/Switzerland

Sister Dr Donna GEERNAERT s.c. (Roman Catholic Church), Canada

Prof. Nicolas LOSSKY (Russian Orthodox Church), France

Bishop (Dr) MAXIMOS of Pittsburgh (Greek Orthodox Archdiocese of North and South America/ Ecumenical Patriarchate), USA

Rev. Dr William G. RUSCH (Evangelical Lutheran Church in America), USA

Rev. Dr Hazel SHERMAN (Baptist Union of Great Britain), England

Dr Mary TANNER (Church of England), England

Rev. Jean TILLARD o.p. (Roman Catholic Church), Canada

Rev. Prof. Dr Dorothea WENDEBOURG (Evangelical Church in Germany), Germany

Staff
Dr Peter BOUTENEFF, Executive Secretary
Rev. Dr Alan D. FALCONER, Director
Mrs Renate SBEGHEN, Administrative Assistant

Apologies
Rt Rev. Dr Samuel AMIRTHAM (Church of South India), India
Rev. Neville CALLAM (Jamaica Baptist Union), Jamaica
Prof. William FRANKLIN (Episcopal Church), USA
Rev. Dr Viorel IONITA (Romanian Orthodox Church), Switzerland